COACH LIKE A MOTHER

A Guide for the 21st Century Sports Coach

Helen M. Williams

COACH LIKE A MOTHER

A Guide for the 21st Century Sports Coach

Helen M. Williams

PEAR TREE PUBLISHING

Coach Like A Mother

By Helen M. Williams
Copyright © 2017 by Helen M. Williams
www.hmwsportsconsulting.com
@hmwspconsulting

Published by Pear Tree Publishing
Bradford, Massachusetts
www.PearTreePublishing.net

No part of this book may be used or reproduced by any means, graphic, electronic, mechanical or by any information storage retrieval system without written permission in writing from the author. No transmittal in any form or by any means allowed without written permission from the author, except in the case of quotations embodied in press, articles and/or reviews.

Second Edition

Published in the United States of America

Williams, Helen M.
    Coach Like a Mother, A Guide for the 21st Century Sports Coach / by Helen M. Williams – 2nd Ed.

    ISBN 978-1-62502-011-6
    Library of Congress Control Number: 2017935984

    1. Basketball–Coaching–United States 2. Coaching–Moral and Ethical Aspects 3. Coaching–Values
    I. Title II. Williams, Helen M.

Sport Balls Clipart by Andresr - http://clipartof.com/222435

Dedication

Everyone is destined to be something. Our destiny is the sum total of life experience. We decide whether we will be the best, be mediocre, or simply be indifferent to that destiny.

I dedicate this book to the most important women in my life; my two mothers Vivian Williams and Cheryl Haynes. Thank you both for being selfless. I hope I have made you proud.

Acknowledgments

There are so many who have helped me succeed in life I fear that I may fall short of thanking them all. With that said I will acknowledge those whose impact I still feel today. I want to thank my birthmother for her courage and for being in my life everyday giving me comfort, counsel, and laughs. Thank you for being brave enough to make an incredibly difficult decision so I could have a good life. Thank you to my brothers Eric and Anthony for never telling me that I couldn't play; Mrs. Kimbro my 11th grade math teacher for empowering me; Julie Soriero for her genuine and intentional thoughtfulness and for giving me an opportunity to pursue a new career path; my stepfather Steve Haynes for teaching me "never be afraid to be a hard act to follow"; Coach Wanda Briley for letting me walk on to the basketball team at Wake Forest; Coach Joe Sanchez for hiring me for my first coaching job; my sisterfriends who tell me what I need to hear and are always available if I need an ear; my players who taught me valuable life lessons in tolerance, patience, and empathy; Sean Frazier for hiring me as a head coach; Vicki Brackens for her financial advice; Women Leaders in College Sports for its support and encouragement; my male and female mentors in athletics; my editor Barry Cohen for helping me be clear in communicating my story; the many people who took the time to read and give me feedback on my manuscript; my publisher Chris Obert for his patience; my angels for guiding and protecting me; the basketball gods who gave me my passion for coaching.

Table of Contents:

Foreword   11

Chapter 1 - WHY DON'T YOU PICK A REAL CAREER?
Seeking happiness   15

Chapter 2 - MAPQUEST VS GPS
How to orchestrate your career   26

Chapter 3 - SCHOOL DAYS
Continuing education   40

Chapter 4 - PHILOSOPHY 101
Preparing for the interview   47

Chapter 5 - I KNOW, BUT…
The mentality of the 21st century kid   51

Chapter 6 - ARE WE THERE YET?
Getting your message through   65

Chapter 7 - AND THE WINNER IS…
Success in recruiting   73

Chapter 8 - WOMAN/MAN IN THE MIRROR
Setting the proper example   81

Chapter 9 - BE WHO WE BE
Developing consistency   87

Chapter 10 - IF MAMA AIN'T HAPPY…
Finding balance   93

Chapter 11 - ARE YOU VISUALLY IMPAIRED?
Visualizing success   102

Chapter 12 - THROW THE BALL TO THE BLUE TEAM!!!
Managing anger and frustration   106

Chapter 13 - SECOND WIND
Avoiding boredom   113

Chapter 14 - TEMPERATURE GAUGE
Assessing the climate of your environment   117

Chapter 15 - FOLLOW THE LEADER
Developing your leadership style   124

Chapter 16 - YES MISS…HOW MAY I HELP YOU TODAY?
Managing people   138

Chapter 17 - COACH, WHAT DOES THIS HAVE TO DO WITH BASKETBALL?
Developing student-athletes   157

Chapter 18 - WOOSAH!
Lessons for life   165

Chapter 19 - PINK SLIP
Dealing with change   170

Chapter 20 - THANKS, COACH!
An attitude of gratitude   183

Resource Guide for Coaches   188
About the Author   190
HMW Sports Consulting   192

Foreword

I first met Helen in the spring of 2011, where she attended one of my workshops. Before I knew her name or her profession it was apparent to me that she was talented, poised, focused and humble. I also knew she had chosen a direction, knew what she wanted and was going to achieve it. Her mission was to learn the things she needed to know to execute her plan smoothly, and to pave the way for a successful transition to her next professional success.

In my experience as a career strategist working with people in all walks of life I have honed my ability to recognize people's strengths quickly. As I got to know Helen I learned she is a results-based leader; a person with passion and a vision, confident in her value system while understanding the importance of listening and leading with purpose. Always a competitor and a planner, Helen constantly looks ahead, asking what she needs to know, what she needs to execute to accomplish her goals. A successful coach who led many, many students to successes of their own, Helen is ever a student herself.

In COACH LIKE A MOTHER Helen is simply doing what she does best, sharing her knowledge in a real and honest way. She discusses the loyalty of coaches, the things that drive them crazy, and the realities of one of the toughest careers people choose. Helen is candid about student-athletes, the ups and downs, the heartache, the tough situations, and planning for success in the ultra-competitive world of sports. She discusses the hard questions and the present climate of 21st century athletics. Her book is refreshing in its frank, straightforward approach.

If you love coaching and aspire to be a great coach, helping student-athletes successfully navigate the competitive world on and off the court, this book is invaluable in determining how to be even more successful in the profession. What separates COACH LIKE A MOTHER is Helen's willingness to share what she has learned through her own journey in order to help others succeed. Helen's story reminds us that successful careers don't just happen. They take hard work, a clear concise plan and consistent execution. Her real stories and insight will not only help you be more successful, they will help you pursue your passion and define yourself in an authentic, meaningful way.

Cindy Key, Career Strategist
Managing Partner and Co-Founder of Key Concepts
www.cdkeyconcepts.com

"Helen is a knowledgeable, experienced professional who is passionate about developing others. She is a visionary with communication skills that enable her to interact successfully with diverse clientele."
Dr. Janice Hilliard-Vice President of Player Development, NBA

"Helen is the consummate sports management professional. Her background as a coach and administrator at Division I, II and III schools uniquely positions her to develop and mentor coaches. In a thoroughly engaging and diplomatic way, she offers advice, gives input, and provides tough feedback."
Cheryl Alexis-Associate Athletic Director, Director of Human Resources, Harvard University

"Helen Williams' seminar for the head coaching staff at UMass Boston was timely, thought provoking and extremely well received by our staff. She is dynamic, honest and captivating as a speaker. If you have the opportunity to engage Helen I assure you that you will find the experience to be delightful and rewarding."
Charlie Titus-Vice Chancellor Athletics Recreation, Special Projects & Programs, UMass Boston

Helen's vast knowledge and experiences were evident as she worked with our coaches. She presents with enthusiasm and sparks great conversations during and after her presentation. We loved her real life approach to all situations. I highly recommend bringing Helen to campus to work with your department.
Andrew Johnson-Director of Athletics, Lehigh Carbon Community College

"Helen's expertise will be very beneficial to anyone wanting to learn the keys to becoming a successful coach and effective leader."
Daynia LaForce-Head Coach, Rhode Island University

Chapter 1
WHY DON'T YOU PICK A REAL CAREER?

I've been writing this book in my head for many years. Every off-season I kept saying I would put it on paper in my spare time. But when do coaches have enough spare time to do anything; much less complete a book? I decided to write this book because there are so many things I wish I knew when I started out as a new coach. I had to learn by doing sometimes--and that didn't always work out so well. It sure would have been nice to at least have something I could refer to for ideas to help form my own philosophy; an operations manual of sorts. I will talk about things throughout the book that worked for me as well as some of my mistakes. And although I am speaking from a college coach's point of view, the content of this book is applicable to coaches at every stage of their career. Any coach of any sport at any level will find something useful by the time they finish reading this. There will be practical and worthwhile information for people new to the profession, as well as those who currently share my passion. You will notice that I dedicated this book to mothers. There is a good reason for that. Mothers are the original coaches. But don't think the title excludes male coaches. Coaching in the 21st century requires new tools for your toolbox and the lessons learned from this book will benefit *ALL* coaches.

I'll start by telling you a little bit about my relationship with sports and how it led to coaching. I grew up in a family of brothers. Being the only girl was a big deal to my mother but I didn't care. I considered myself an athlete and to me there was no distinction between male and female. Whatever my brothers did, wherever they went, I followed. One of my first memories is of asking my mother why I couldn't run outside and play in the sun with my shirt off like my brothers. I thought my chest was identical to theirs so I saw no reason to have to wear a shirt in the hot sun! I was a good athlete and capable of doing all the stuff the neighborhood boys do, so I played whatever games they played. I felt like I belonged in sports simply because I hung out with my brothers and they never told me I couldn't play.

> "I felt like I belonged in sports simply because I hung out with my brothers and they never told me I couldn't play."

Much to my mother's dismay I loved sports. She wanted me to "act like a girl" but I was intent on just being me. Every Saturday she would get exasperated when I would leave the beauty parlor in the morning with a perfect ponytail and come home that afternoon with my hair all over my head "lookin' a hot mess". I can't tell you how many arguments we had about me being a tomboy and her wanting me to wear dresses to school. But I just wanted to play ball. As soon as I got home from school and finished my homework I was out the door in my "play clothes" ready to play whatever games we made up.

One time in junior high my mom told me not to go to an away game because she had to work and couldn't pick me up when I returned. I protested and tried to explain to her that you can't just not show up for a game when you play on a team. She didn't understand and told me I had better come home after school. This was the one and only time I deliberately defied my mother. I knew when I got on that bus that I was going to be in a whole lot of trouble but I just had to play. When I got home I got my butt whipped but it was worth it.

My house was on a street in what I would consider a regular neighborhood. Each house had a front and back yard. Some driveways were paved and others were gravel. A few homes had garages for their cars and chairs on the porches for people to watch whomever drove up and down the street. We had a basketball rim nailed to a tree in our backyard. I played hoops with my brothers so much the grass stopped growing and there was only dirt after a while. On rainy days we couldn't play because the ball wouldn't bounce in the mud. There were always plenty of kids in my age group to hang around with and we played every sport you can imagine. I lived close enough to my school that if I missed the bus and had to walk I could still get there on time. Along the way there was a park where I could stop and play ball on my way home each afternoon. At that time you could wander the neighborhood alone all day and parents didn't have to worry about people snatching their kids in broad daylight. The only rule from my mother was that we had "better be home before the street lights came on". There was also a park about four streets over in the opposite direction from my house. We could play there, but a lot of times we just played games in the street. You took your life in your hands if you played wide receiver in football games because you had to keep your eye on the ball while simultaneously trying to avoid the parked cars. Of course there is always a neighborhood home where all the kids gravitate to play. For me that was Earl Hoke's house up the street from where I lived. His was the only one on the block with a real basketball goal on a concrete driveway. We spent hours in his backyard shooting hoops, making sure the ball never touched the laundry ever present on the clothesline to the left of the basketball goal. For some reason his goal was 11 feet high instead of the standard 10 feet so I developed a very funky shooting form to compensate for that--and to get my shot over the arms of the taller, older boys I played with. I didn't know until I got to college that my shooting form was wrong because, except for junior high and high school, I never had any formal coaching.

When I was growing up Title IX had been passed into law, but it was not always adhered to by everyone. Amateur Athletic Union (AAU) teams were not the huge organizations with a team for every age group that are commonplace today. I was always drawn to basketball because (like most team sports) it involved everybody and didn't single out one person. If you were just an okay player you could still play and enjoy the game. You blended in and nobody would know whether you could or could not shoot or dribble. I don't remember ever being the last one picked begrudgingly or being given any special treatment because I was the only girl. I could play and that's all the guys and I ever cared about. I could compete so I was accepted. It's as simple as that. To this day that experience helped shaped my perception of my ability to achieve whatever I set my mind to do. Even now the confidence I gained on those fields and courts helps guide me.

I got involved in coaching because I *love* what sports did for me. I wanted to be able to return the favor and help other kids. I am the person I have become because of my experience in athletics. I lost both my parents by the time I was 15 and basketball saved my life. Had it not been for that orange ball and my books I may have ended up on drugs, pregnant, in jail, or conceivably all three. After my parents died athletics and academics kept me sane. I had always loved reading books and was a good student in most subjects with the exception of math (although I will tell you later why my math teacher was my favorite). I also loved throwing any kind of ball.

Basketball was the one thing that made me like all the other kids. In team sports everyone is the same. You wear the same gear, the same shoes, etc. No one knows that you can't afford the latest style polo shirt or sneakers. No one knows that when you go home you're not sure if you will have heat in the winter or food in the refrigerator. Somehow I came to the conclusion that education was my way out. I have no memory of it, but the only explanation for that I can think of is I must have had conversations with my mother about the importance of a college degree. I knew if I studied hard I could go to college and that it would change my life. So I was happy to get up in the morning and go to school and even happier at the end of the day when I would get to go to practice. And I knew that I would never, ever want to stop playing basketball.

When I walked on at Wake Forest University I had not been recruited. But I made the squad because I was a fast athlete, a really good defender, loved to pass the ball, and I worked hard. I *never* got playing time in college. In fact, I can remember every point I ever scored (which tells you how much I did *not* play!). After two decades of coaching I realized that if I had been the coach I wouldn't have played me either. But none of that mattered to me. What did matter was that I had coaches and teammates who were my family and with whom I would have a lifetime bond. I can call my teammates or coach anytime, start a conversation and it's like we never left school.

There was a girl named Amy Privette (now Amy Perko, the Executive Director of the Knight Commission on Intercollegiate Athletics) that came to Wake the same year I did. We were the only two freshmen and we couldn't have been more polar opposites. She was White; I was Black. She was recruited and I was a walk on. She had two parents; I did not. She played 40 minutes every game. I sat at the end of the bench. I always thought Amy was so lucky. But the wonderful thing about her was that she thought so too. Amy was an incredible teammate. One thing about our relationship will always stay with me. Once we were at a tournament getting dressed after a game and I was distraught because I didn't get to play. As usual Amy played well and had been selected the MVP. She saw how depressed I was, came over to me and said "You can have this trophy. You deserve it for all the hard work you put in." I've had that trophy since 1983. That's the kind of thing that makes being on a team a blessing and one of many reasons I will always be involved with athletics.

I learned many life skills as a teammate that on my own I wouldn't have otherwise acquired at such a young age. On my first day of practice in college I was terrified because I didn't know if I would be able to make it through a four-hour practice. (In those days there were no mandatory days off or 20 hour time limits). But I made it through that practice and many more. Those hours of preparation helped me realize I could be tough and fight through adversity. I learned how important it was to do my part to make the team successful; that anything in life worth having is never easy; that I could succeed at anything if I just put my mind to it. The great thing about sports is they teach you life skills that prepare you for the real world. As an athlete I learned leadership skills, problem solving, strategic thinking, teamwork, commitment, interpersonal and communication skills, accountability, responsibility, sportsmanship, navigating adversity, and adjusting to change. I probably would have learned those lessons eventually through trial and error, but I'm positive that had I not been on a team it would mostly have been by error.

I became a coach because of my love for the game. I also never wanted a "real job". I wanted to enjoy what I did and had the audacity to think I could get paid for it. Some people work at a job because they have no choice and need to make an honest living. But I had enough part time jobs in college to know that I never wanted to get up in the morning and dread going to work. Coaching gives me that. Not one day of my athletic career have I gotten up and not wanted to go to work because I didn't like what I do. And it's cool to get paid for it.

I believe it is a privilege to coach because I have the ability to help change a kid's life and I take that responsibility seriously. Offering a kid an opportunity to break the negative cycle of a family should never be taken lightly. I realize a scholarship that provides an education for a student-athlete can also help transform future generations of his or her family. And I get an enormous amount of joy from the looks of relief and gratitude that I have seen on the faces of parents when they know their child has a chance at a better life. The importance of a college scholarship is ingrained on me because I didn't have one. I borrowed money and received financial aid to pay for my four years at Wake Forest and two years of graduate school because I couldn't afford it any other way. Today I would do the same thing because it was something I wanted and I essentially invested in myself. But college is expensive in the 21st century. When I was a freshman at Wake my entire bill was $7,500. By the time I graduated it had risen to $10,000 and I thought that was outrageous. A college education today can cost five times that amount. It took me 20 years to pay back my loans. Helping a kid avoid that kind of debt is one of the things that still drives me today.

The game has allowed me to experience so many wonderful things. I have traveled all over the United States and to places overseas. Sports helped broaden my perspective of life so that I didn't have a myopic view of the world. And though all coaches wish they could reach more kids, I know I have impacted some in a positive manner. Coaching is a noble profession. It's so much more than just rolling the ball out onto the gym floor or onto the field. With this book I strive to continue giving back to the game by sharing my thoughts and experiences with other coaches. I hope to continue being a part of helping even more kids benefit from sports the way I did.

What I relate in the following chapters is simply *my* experience at coaching college basketball for over two decades. When I retired from coaching I realized that new coaches are never actually taught how to be successful. They are simply given a whistle and told "Welcome to coaching!" Not everything I talk about will be pretty. But if you're going to coach on any level you need to hear the real story. Some of my thoughts are timeless and others will change with the times. But the basic premise remains the same. People who coach love it. We're crazy for doing it and we are passionate. I doubt any of us who made the choice to coach for the right reasons would trade it for anything.

Chapter 2
MAPQUEST VS GPS

Once you decide to coach you must then chart your course. Sometimes that course will be guided by what you see (i.e. MapQuest paper directions) and sometimes you have to trust what you are being told by people who care about you and want you to succeed (i.e. GPS). Be mindful of the totality of your career. Are you driving the process of your growth/career, rather than letting it happen arbitrarily? What is your ultimate goal? Do you want to be a head coach or career assistant? On what level do you want to coach? Do you have goals with measurable outcomes? Once you determine those goals you will need to figure out how to best navigate each step. Let's look at a few important items on your "to do" list.

> "Be mindful of the totality of your career. Are you driving the process of your growth/career, rather than letting it happen arbitrarily?"

Hone Your Skills. There are so many responsibilities in coaching that have nothing to do with x's and o's. If you're going to be a successful coach in the 21st century, you must have a complete skill set. Be sure as an assistant you get involved in every aspect of running a program. Don't just be a recruiter or labeled as proficient in only one aspect of coaching. When I was an assistant at Wake Forest I was asked to do scouting reports for the first time. My job was to let the head coach know every strength and weakness of our opponents. At that time we could do live scouts so I went to games at least three times a week because I didn't know how to watch games with a critical eye. It wasn't like it is now where coaches get the games on TV or the web and they have the benefit of the ability to rewind and replay. I really had to learn to process trends on the fly and it was the first time I was forced out of my comfort zone. When you become a head coach, not everything will be a strength. That's why you hire assistants. But you still need to know what's going on in order to make sure your assistants are doing their jobs. Ask for and/or create learning experiences so you are fully prepared.

Expand Your Knowledge Base. It's always great to learn new things. For assistants, it's great to bring new techniques to your head coach so they know you are striving to develop. If you are a head coach, occasionally changing your routine keeps practice fresh. There are many ways you can do this and I will discuss them in a later chapter.

Don't Be Picky About The Level If You Want To Be A Head Coach. If you have an opportunity to be a head coach and feel you are ready, do it, regardless of the level. It doesn't matter if it's Div I, II, III, NAIA, JUCO, or High School. I always told recruits the x's and o's are the same. Competition is relative. "Get in where you fit in". Each level has championships and trophies. I took a pay cut with my first head coaching job. It was a decision I don't regret because I finally got an opportunity to run my own program. A lot of coaches are caught in a catch-22. Athletic Directors (ADs) won't hire you because you don't have head coaching experience but you can't get head coaching experience unless they hire you! You can be somewhat selective but don't be too picky and cost yourself an opportunity to prove you have the ability to be successful sitting in the "big chair".

Expand Your Pedigree Geographically. When I first started coaching I wanted to make sure I learned from as many people as possible and use that information to form my own philosophy. After I finished graduate school I returned to my alma mater Wake Forest to work for my former coach, Joe Sanchez. I worked full time on a 10-month contract for only $10,000 but I didn't care. I was coaching at a Division I institution in the ACC and I knew it would benefit me later. Two years later I decided that I needed to get away from Wake Forest. I had spent six years there as a player and coach and wanted new experiences. That year I ran into Trudi Lacey at the NCAA Final Four Championship. She had made a great impression on me when she lectured at one of our summer camps at Wake. We talked, she mentioned she was looking for an assistant, and I told her I was ready to move on. So I moved to the University of South Florida. After two years in the Southeast I literally got out a map, said "Where have I not lived?", and twirled it around. Then I closed my eyes and stuck my index finger on the map. It landed in the Midwest. So that year I went to the Final Four looking for a job in the Midwest. At one of the banquets I was alone looking for a place to sit. I saw an empty chair next to Pat Charity, the head coach at Western Michigan University. I asked if anyone was sitting next to her. She was saving the seat for someone else but they hadn't arrived so she said I was free to sit down. During our conversation, I told her I was looking to move to the Midwest. She needed an assistant and that's how I ended up at Western Michigan. I spent four years at Western Michigan before Coach Sanchez asked me to join him at the US Naval Academy. Those five wonderful years at Navy were some of my favorite coaching days. I always had a healthy respect for the military because my father and brothers served in the Army, and I nearly went to Officer Candidate School myself after college. Being the "third leg" of the proverbial "stool", as the Commandant often referred to the education of the Midshipmen, was a privilege. It was a joy to witness the development of the men and women who will be leading this country in the future. It is awesome now to see how some of the players I coached have risen in the ranks of the Navy and Marines.

  I had several unsuccessful head coaching interviews while I was at Navy. Frustrated after 15 years of coaching and those failed attempts, I decided to save my money for the next year and leave the profession. I made my peace with God and figured He had something else in store for me. So I went recruiting in July, determined to give my best effort for one more year. At an AAU tournament, I ran into Richard Barron from Princeton University. He mentioned that he had an opening for an assistant and gave me his card. I gave the card to a friend that I knew was looking for a job! Little did I know Richard was planting a seed. And here's why luck sometimes plays a key part in your career. At another tournament later that July I had gone to a gym to watch a player and, unbeknownst to me, the schedule had been changed. I decided to stay at that gym anyway and watch the next game. At halftime I stepped outside to thaw out (because all AAU games have to be played in air conditioned gyms) and ran into Richard again. He asked me once more if I would be interested in his opening. Part of me wanted to say no because I had applied for the head job at Princeton and didn't even get a response. But Richard was very persuasive and asked if we could just go to dinner and talk about it. I went from "Are you interested?" at 11:00 am to "When can you start?" by 7:00 pm. Be grateful when divine intervention plays a part in your life.

In my fourth and final year at Princeton we tied for the regular season conference championship with Dartmouth and Brown. At that time the Ivy League did not have a postseason tournament. The automatic bid went to the regular season champion so we were in a three-way playoff. We won the coin toss, got a bye, and would play the Sunday afternoon game. On Friday night I was in my office listening to the game on the Internet and working on my scout when I got a phone call. When the phone rang I thought "Who would be calling my office this time of night?" When I answered it was Sean Frazier calling. His exact words were "I'm the AD at Merrimack College and I'm calling to make you my next Head Coach". I thought "Who is this?" But he was serious and I got my first head coaching job after many years as an assistant. I promise it really happened that way. But I don't want to give the false impression that it was easy. I had to work very hard and do my job well to put myself in position to take advantage of each opportunity. If you're lucky enough to be at a big-time program and learn under a current or future Hall of Fame coach it's great. But if you're like me, someone not well known, who never played, and didn't have connections coming out of college, sometimes you might have to work harder to get that first opportunity. So it's important to make sure you have varied experiences on your resume. The key is to never turn down an opportunity unless you have a good reason (i.e. children, etc). And *never* take a coaching job for the money. The places I coached were not necessarily ones I would have picked myself. I'm from the South and hate cold weather, but the opportunities in Michigan and Massachusetts were too good to pass up and I knew working at both places would help my career.

Take Advantage of the Knowledge of the Administrative Staff In Your Department. ADs and Associate/Assistant ADs are great resources to help further your career. First of all, they see you work every day and will be great references when you apply for jobs. Second, the good ones have your best interest at heart and want to help you develop. I'm very thankful to Mike Cross who was the Asst. AD at Princeton when I coached there because he assisted me in my preparation for the interview that would lead to my first head coaching job. After I was unsuccessful in a previous interview he asked if I could use his help. The suggestions he gave me were simple, yet crucial to my interviewing skills. The one thing he told me that sticks out in my memory is, "You are the expert on you". How simple is that? But the light bulb turned on in my head with those few words. I realized that I had not done an adequate job of selling myself in interviews and that's probably why I had not been successful at getting a head coaching job. A lot of coaches fail to give a complete picture of their accomplishments. Sometimes it's because we don't think about it; other times it's because we don't know how. You may need to get help telling your story on paper with your resume or in person. ADs will be a great resource for your preparation because they are the ones involved in the hiring process. Don't overlook the help that is only a few doors down the hallway.

Build Relationships. Most people refer to this as networking, but what does that really mean? It's important to develop relationships of all types in any profession, but the world of coaching is especially small. Every person you meet knows someone who knows someone who knows someone. This applies to all sports. So much of the information acquired about job openings circulates before the position is even posted. In fact, by the time it's posted the top candidates are probably already in play. An AD once introduced me to the concept of "social capital". This means you have to invest in developing relationships consistently and build connections with people who are going to advocate for you and help move your career forward.

There are a few important factors to remember about the relationships you develop. First, don't limit your contacts to coaches. Include all types of people in the athletic department and at the university. This will be very important in planning your post coaching career. Administrators talk. Sports Information Directors talk. Professors talk. Equipment managers, interns, and athletic trainers talk. Don't overlook anyone. When you research jobs you want to be able to get the complete picture so you need all the help you can get. Second, be genuine in your relationships. Don't just collect business cards. Work to give as well as get something from relationships. Being fake won't get you very far. I remember when I started in coaching I didn't realize how disingenuous I was being when I networked. My goal was to collect business cards from everyone I met and use them later as contacts. One Final Four I embarrassed myself at a seminar about networking. Someone was explaining the importance of it and I got up to make a comment because I wanted to be noticed. I told the audience of coaches that you should introduce yourself and talk to head coaches. I said "It doesn't matter what you say. Make up stuff so you can converse with them." I still cringe when I remember that, even though it was over two decades ago. Finally, don't blow off young coaches who come to you for help or seeking advice. I've always admired and taken a special interest in those coaches who have taken the initiative to introduce themselves. If they make an effort to talk to me I make sure and listen because everyone is important. Remember the six degrees of separation theory? You never know how important the person sitting next to you will be in your life.

Bloom Where You Are Planted. The best job you have is the one where you are. If you spend all your time looking for the next opportunity you won't do the job you have very well. One of the greatest lessons I learned while working at the US Naval Academy was their philosophy on leadership. You must learn to follow before you can become a good leader. Their motto "Honor, Courage, and *Commitment*" still rings true for me today. Thinking the grass is greener on the other side can get you in trouble. A favorite quote of mine is from a woman named Betty Furness who said "Do any job you are doing well and you'll stumble over the opportunity to do what you truly desire." When I mentioned earlier about moving around I didn't mean that the time you spend at one job should be set in stone because you should think about your future. But be patient. You'll know when you have absorbed all you can and need to move on. In the meantime, make sure not to shortchange the people or kids you work with.

> "I dressed not for where I was but for where I wanted to be –a head coach. I looked the part before I got the part."

Learn Something From Every Head Coach You Work For. It's important you take something to use from everyone with whom you work. Otherwise your experience in their presence was wasted. Each head coach I worked for taught me something different. I learned from Coach Sanchez to take care of your assistants. I was barely making any money but he took care of me in other ways. He arranged for me to have meals in the cafeteria at Wake Forest and his wife had me over for dinner almost every night. He helped me find an apartment on campus that I could afford. And when I went scouting he always paid for my meals or gas. From Trudi Lacey I learned the importance of image. She taught me that you represent your program, department, and institution every time you step out in public. So I began to make sure that I looked presentable at all times. I dressed not for where I was but for where I wanted to be –a head coach. I looked the part before I got the part. Pat Charity taught me the importance of caring about your players off the court or field. She helped me understand that it's a coach's responsibility to help players develop into well-rounded citizens who make positive contributions to society. And Richard Barron taught me the importance of allowing your assistants to do their job without micromanaging, giving them new responsibilities to help them grow in the profession. One other critical point to consider is that it is just as important to learn what *not* to do in coaching. Sometimes that is an even more valuable lesson. So if you are in a situation that you are not happy with, use that as a "teachable moment". Don't "sleep" on the job. Take in all the information you can.

Develop Your Critical Skills. These skills are personal attributes that enhance an individual's interactions with others. They relate to a person's ability to have positive interpersonal relationships with coworkers, the people they report to, the people they supervise, etc. Examples of these include communication skills, work ethic, ability to collaborate and problem solve, self-confidence, adaptability and conflict management. As we all know perception can be reality and your ability to show proficiency in these skills that are not easily quantifiable but recognizable is extremely important.

Become Proficient At Fundraising. During uncertain economic times, private and public universities have trimmed their budgets and asked athletic departments to carry more of their own weight. Having the ability to understand fundraising within the context of your institution's goals and plans will make you a valuable asset to your athletic department.

Make sure you monitor your professional development. Many times we coaches don't spend enough time developing and preparing ourselves for life after coaching. I paid a heavy price when I made the mistake of talking about being an administrator after I finished coaching, but never doing anything to prepare myself for it. Fortunately, through my relationship building I was offered an opportunity to take an accelerated internship at Massachusetts Institute of Technology and a Fellowship at Harvard University. I had to squeeze a lot of learning into a limited time period.

Have a purpose. Have a plan and work that plan. Do what we tell our players to do. Look down the road and know where you want to be in 20 or 30 years. Figure out what new skills you need to acquire and what relationships you need to develop and cultivate. Otherwise you will look up one day and realize you've been running in place with nothing to show for it.

Chapter 3
SCHOOL DAYS

Our kids aren't the only ones who need to improve. Every coach can learn something new that will help him or her grow. Coaches need coaching too! The moment you think you know it all is the moment you set yourself up for failure. All coaches make mistakes at crucial times in a game or in dealing with players. It's not fun going through the process but it is beneficial because that is how we get better. And every great coach will tell you that if they evaluate themselves at the end of each season there will always be something they need to work on. Here are some areas coaches should spend time developing:

> "The moment you think you know it all is the moment you set yourself up for failure."

EDUCATION Having a college degree is one thing that may keep you from being eliminated early in a job search; especially for a head coaching job. The ads will say "bachelor's degree required, master's degree preferred", but it is an unwritten rule that head coaches have their master's degree because, first and foremost, we are educators. Equally important, you should find ways to visibly let your kids know you will always make academics a priority in your life. Show them that continuing education is an important part of your professional development.

SPORT KNOWLEDGE There are many ways to improve at learning and teaching the game:

1. **Attend your sport's national convention.** Lots of coaches think their convention is an opportunity to blow off steam/stress from the season and relax away from our players. We spend time commiserating about the ups and downs of the season with our friends who we may only get to see once a year. We hang out and decompress. But we should also take advantage of all that great knowledge in one place. It can be formal (seminars) or informal (getting together with a group of coaches and sharing drills, etc). Make it a point to talk to other coaches, watch open practices, and bring new things back to enhance your program.

2. **Watch games.** (Men's and women's, professional and collegiate) during the regular season and playoffs with pen and pad in hand. It's so hard for me to just "watch" a game

on TV after becoming a head coach. Even now in my career as a broadcaster I always find some new play or defense that I would have incorporated into my system. Sometimes you learn a lot and see things that will help you grow just by watching or listening to a different coaching philosophy. The time period from January through the first week of April has always been my favorite time of year because there is a basketball game at some level broadcast every night of the week. When I am home from work or relaxing on the weekend I still turn on the TV and try to absorb as much basketball as I can. With all the sports channels available today your sport will undoubtedly be televised at some point. Don't waste that free opportunity.

3. **Watch the practices of your counterpart.** I can't tell you how many drills I have taken from men's practices as an assistant and a head coach and used them with my teams. It helped add variety to our practice and made me a better coach. Also, don't limit your learning only to coaches in your own sport. One time I couldn't get my players to understand how I wanted them to throw an outlet pass on the fast break. The type of pass I wanted reminded me of what a quarterback throws to his receivers. So I went to our football coach, asked him what he taught his players, and took the drill back to my basketball practice.

4. **Review game film from the previous year with another coach.** Every summer I grabbed a couple of game films and watch them with a coaching buddy. Inevitably s/he saw things that should have been obvious to me that I missed or gave me tips to improve my system. Having another set of eyes is always beneficial.

5. **Evaluate yourself at the end of every year to see where you need to get better, and then find someone to teach you.** As a head coach I would look at what I needed to work on, find out who the expert in that area was, then call and ask them if I could come talk. I visited men's and women's staffs from different sports and watched them do workouts, got new drills and talked to them about what they did in their programs that made them successful. Most of the coaches didn't know me from Adam but they always obliged when I asked to come visit. Coaches are willing to spend time with you if you just ask. In my entire career not one coach I asked for help ever turned me down.

PUBLIC SPEAKING This is an area I think coaches neglect (and oftentimes avoid) because some of us just aren't that good at it (or we have an inflated sense of our ability). But it's an important skill that could mean the difference between getting a job or not. Being articulate is important in a whole host of areas (recruiting, fundraising, community service, etc) that reflect on your program, department and institution. If you have a fear of public speaking then you need to get over it. ADs have to "win the press conference" when they hire head coaches and that's not going to be you if they don't feel you can address the community (especially boosters and donors) in an intelligent and articulate manner. Ways to improve:

1. **Volunteer at your convention.** Be a presenter or moderator. It's great practice in front of a fairly friendly crowd (your peers).

2. **Volunteer to speak to community groups.** Plenty of people want you to talk to their kids. They see coaches as role models and would jump at the chance to have you speak. You may eventually get paid if you become proficient at it.

3. **Public speaking classes.** Many schools allow employees to take classes for free or at reduced cost. Take a class at your school during the summer session before or after your recruiting period. Also, many communities offer great non-credit adult education classes at the local community

college. And talking about the classes you take to your players is a visible way of demonstrating to them your commitment to education.

4. **Toastmasters International.** This is an organization that helps people learn how to write and prepare speeches. They meet periodically to work on public speaking and leadership skills. It's good because it helps you learn to think on your feet. Find the chapter nearest you.

WRITING This is a skill most people think they do well, but it's one we all can improve on. Writing comes into play with cover letters, emails/letters to recruits, Twitter and Facebook posts, blogs, and even replies to administrators' memos. It helps get your name out there and shows that you are knowledgeable about your sport. One important thing to note: *please* make sure you use appropriate English in traditional communications and not text message or twitter language!

1. **Submit articles to professional journals.** These include NABC, WBCA, AFCA, AVCA, NCAA publications, web magazines, blogs, etc. This is a great way to introduce yourself to the public.

2. **Write a newsletter for your team.** It's a fun way to get information out about your program.

COMMITTEES Serving on committees is a great educational tool for coaches. It helps you understand the processes that lead to policy and rule changes. Often as coaches we are on the receiving end of regulations without an understanding of the debate and rationale that lead to their passage. Serving on campus committees is a great way to develop positive relationships with faculty and staff. It's also an opportunity to integrate your program with the university. People will see that you are not just a "dumb jock"; that we coaches are cerebral and do have thoughts and opinions on things other than sports. Your service allows them to see that you care about and are invested in the mission of the university. This helps them understand that the athletic department adds value to the university, rather than being viewed as "those people over there in athletics".

Don't be a hypocrite when it comes to promoting education. We work at places where the mandate is to educate students. We tell our players all the time how important it is to make academics a priority so we should be examples for them. This is one area where the "Do as I say, not as I do" philosophy won't fly.

Chapter 4
PHILOSOPHY 101

When head coaches interview for jobs they have an official record of their coaching and leadership ability. But as an assistant you really have no track record of success on your own so you must be able to demonstrate to an AD how you will be successful. One of the ways I prepared for interviews was to develop my own dossier of ideas and philosophy so that I could show something concrete to the people I interviewed with and they would see that I had a plan. I created a power point presentation because I realized that when I spoke from memory, I left out many important aspects about myself and my philosophy when people asked me questions. Make sure you include the following things:

WHO ARE YOU?
You are the expert on you. Let them know who you are and what you value.

STATEMENT OF COACHING PHILOSOPHY
Why are you coaching? What are your goals in the profession?

FIVE YEAR PLAN

(Include your philosophy in each area)
1. Recruiting
2. Academics
3. Community Relations
4. Fundraising
5. Alumni Relations
6. Marketing/Promotions
7. Player Development
8. Staff Development
9. Scheduling
10. Budget Analysis

STAFF REQUIREMENTS

(Include how you envision assigning duties)

Head Coach

1st Assistant Coach

2nd Assistant Coach

Graduate Assistant Coach

Director of Basketball Operations

TWELVE-MONTH ACTIVITY PLAN

What do you plan to accomplish each month in your first year?

TEAM POLICY MANUAL

(The players call it a rule book!)

What are your standards in the areas of Academics, Attire, Alcohol, Drugs, Smoking, Curfew, Social Media, Team Decorum, Cell Phones, Media, Parent Etiquette, and other areas of concern to your program?

DEFENSIVE/OFFENSIVE PHILOSOPHY

Be descriptive. Use the dry erase board in your interview. Show that you are knowledgeable and have executive presence.

PRACTICE PHILOSOPHY

Daily Team/Individual Practice Components

5-Week Preseason Practice Plan
(Weeks 1-5 with daily schedule)

Weekly In Season Practice Plans
(Weeks 1-4 with daily schedule)

SCOUTING/GAME PREPARATION

How will you make sure your team is fully prepared to compete? (Note that these areas are specific to basketball but you can apply the same principles to any sport.)

It's important you develop your philosophy while you are an assistant if you want to become a head coach. As I've mentioned before I think it's a good idea to work for more than one person so you don't always view the game through a narrow lens. Take something from each head coach and figure out what you want to do when you sit in the big chair.

But remember, getting the job is not the end. It's merely the beginning. Now you have to put into practice all that you've written

> "Dealing with 18-22 year olds requires that you understand life happens in the gray area."

and thought about. Everything won't always work like you envision it will. It took me a long time to realize that in coaching everything is not black and white. Dealing with 18-22 year olds requires that you understand life happens in the gray area.

When you move that one inch over to the big chair you'll realize it's not the same. You can only prepare so much. Some things you're just going to have to experience to learn. And your stress will increase exponentially because there will be a whole new level of responsibility and accountability. But that's okay. The beauty of it all comes when you do finally "get it". And *that* is a great feeling.

Chapter 5

I KNOW, BUT...

Coaching 21st century kids is a huge challenge. I'm sure I sound like my mom when I say "they don't make 'em like they used to" is apropos. It's not like "back in the day" when I played. Kids are a different breed in the 21st century. For the most part kids have changed because society has changed. Not all kids work hard because they understand that's what it takes to succeed. Many of them expect a quick return on their efforts because instant gratification is how they live. It's the "microwave mentality". Everyone has a Smartphone and they have grown up with everything immediately available at their fingertips. Push a button and get an instant result on social media. They use Google to research something instead of going to the library. As a result, this is how they approach life. Their thinking is "I know I only worked hard for three weeks but I should start. I know I didn't do any conditioning over the summer but you shouldn't hold that against me. I know I didn't work to improve my game in the off-season but you shouldn't take me out of the game after a few turnovers". Those of us with a little age realize that life doesn't work that way and we constantly struggle to communicate this to our kids.

A classic example of the "I know, but..." mentality is a conversation I had after I decided to check the class of one of my players. Her class began at 12:00 so I stopped by on my way to lunch. I arrived at 11:50 and waited in front of her classroom. She didn't show up until 12:05.

"What time does your class start?"

"12:00."

"What time does my Blackberry say?"

"12:05."

"What's wrong with this picture? Why are you late?"

"I had to print out a report. My printer wasn't working yesterday."

"Why didn't you just go to the library and print it out?"

"It was late and the library was closed."

"Why didn't you print it out this morning?"

"Coach, you had practice this morning and I didn't have time."

"What you are really telling me is that you waited until the last minute and didn't plan."

"But Coach, I was only five minutes late! And the professor is never on time anyway."

"In the real world, if you work on Wall Street and you are five minutes late making trades for your clients you potentially cost them millions of dollars. And it just so happens that today the professor was early to class. So I ask you again, 'what's wrong with this picture?'"

My players hated when I gave them real world analogies because they are so used to not being held accountable and they figure things will always get worked out for them.

The "I know, but…" mentality starts with society being so worried about a child's psyche that they are not allowed to experience any growth from being challenged. No one is supposed to feel left out or "less than" another so we have soccer games where everyone is supposed to play, no score is kept and everyone gets a trophy for participation. It's frowned upon if anyone is left behind. That might be okay for itty-bitty kids. But for older kids it hinders development into independent beings and doesn't teach "real life" lessons. Everyone has been telling them all their lives they are the best thing since sliced bread and when they get to college they don't understand why you don't give them the same treatment. One kid goes home and only eats Burger King over the summer, gains 15 pounds and is out of shape when s/he comes back in the fall. Another one ignores the sprints you put in his or her summer workout and comes back unable to complete a preseason run. Really all we are asking them to do is work to reach their full potential. In the real world, if you do your job well, then maybe, just maybe, you get a pat on the back. But 21st century kids want that pat on the back *before they do anything*. Earning praise is not something they are used to. It's a constant struggle to teach them what waits in the real world. Let's review some of the things we struggle to deal with when coaching kids of the 21st century:

Temptations and Distractions. It's tough growing up for kids in the 21st century. They are exposed to so much more than when I was a kid. They see so many negative things on TV and in movies. Video games celebrate violence. Reality shows have the highest ratings on TV but could not be further from actual reality. Some kids don't have a stable home life with parents who care enough to discipline them. Some have parents who struggle to put food on the table, clothes on their backs and a roof over their heads, so there's not much time for individual attention. And *every* kid has a cell phone permanently attached to his or her fingertips (you will notice I didn't say ears because kids of the 21st century rarely "talk" on the phone). There's also the distraction of relationships. It's crazy, but a kid's performance on a particular day could hinge on their relationship with a significant other. They can have a bad game because they broke up or got into an argument. The worst part is that you may not find out until after the game what's wrong with them (if you find out at all).

Lack of Interpersonal Skills. 21st century kids don't enjoy face to face communication. The closest they get to that is Skype, FaceTime, or YouTube. If they can't express themselves via social media they don't want to communicate. Kids struggle to look you in the eye and have a heart to heart conversation if something is bothering them. They would rather discuss or vent issues electronically because it's easier and they can hide behind their words. And don't mention trying to pry them away from the video games! That's the only thing that holds their attention for extended periods of time.

The lines of authority have also been blurred for them. They think it is okay to refer to authority figures by their first name. I always told my players they would only be allowed to call me by my first name when they received their college degree. Today, years after graduating college, I still have too much respect for my college coaches to call them by their first names. It works for some people but it just doesn't sound right to me.

Communication Styles. People process information differently. Some people are visual learners. They need to see things to understand. Some are auditory learners. They can hear what you say and comprehend. Some are kinesthetic learners. They have to feel things (in other words, they have to physically be walked through things to understand). I am a visual learner by nature and I think most freshmen are that way. When my kids asked me questions in practice I had them show me on the floor where they were confused. It's only from two decades of experience that I developed the ability to process information through the other methods. It took me a while to realize that you can say one thing to a group of kids and they all process it differently; that you may have to communicate different ways to different people in order for them to understand. It doesn't mean a kid is stupid. But you need to make sure you know the sport IQ of your team because you may have to adjust your coaching to help each kid be successful. I tried to make sure I used all three types of communication on a daily basis.

Over Scheduling. Kids of all ages don't have free time. They don't "play" anymore. Everything they do is scheduled. They either have training or practice and are always being driven somewhere or guided through some activity. Kids don't come home, put on their play clothes and go outside to play until it gets dark. When I was young we made up games to keep ourselves occupied. We decided what the rules were going to be and if there was an issue we policed ourselves and solved our own problems. When we picked teams we had a strategy. We weren't told that the teams had to be even. We picked people for our team we thought we had a chance to win with. Today kids have trouble picking teams to play pickup because someone else has always decided what team they should be on. Very rarely do they have time to catch their breath, recharge and just be "kids". Not having spontaneous time to themselves and with each other keeps them from naturally developing the problem solving and interpersonal skills they will need as adults.

Specialization. I am a firm believer that kids should play every sport they like at least until they become juniors in high school. Then, if they are talented enough to get a scholarship, maybe they should focus on one thing. But parents today start training their kids when they are still in elementary school. A lot of little kids have personal trainers by the time they get to middle school. That can lead to burnout or injuries and it might happen by the time they get to you.

Overbearing Parents. One of the toughest things to get kids to do today is be self-sufficient. Helicopter Parents hover over their kids and do everything for them. Kids are not asked to do things on their own that will help them be independent. I

"Parents don't allow kids to fail anymore. Failure is one of life's greatest teaching tools..."

coached one kid who had never mailed a letter. She didn't even know how to go to the post office and get a stamp! I could not believe that she had never performed such a routine task. When I asked her why she didn't know how she told me her mom always mailed things for her. So I told her "Get an envelope. In the center of the envelope write the address of the person you are sending it to. In the upper left hand corner put your address. Go to the post office and buy a stamp, either from the machine or the postal worker behind the counter. Place the stamp in the upper right hand corner of the envelope. Then put the letter in the chute marked for outgoing mail." Unbelievable but true. Now there is a new breed of Lawnmower Parents who remove all obstacles to spare their children from adverse experiences.

Parents don't allow kids to fail anymore. Failure is one of life's greatest teaching tools, but 21st century kids aren't allowed to fall so they don't learn how to get up, figuratively speaking. Our kids' lack of ability to bounce back from failure is one of the biggest problems in this country. Parents need to take the "training wheels" off and let their children grow up. Sometimes when my players asked a question I would not give them help even if I knew the answer. I would tell them to "figure it out" because I wanted to empower them with the confidence that they could make good decisions.

Too Much Testing. There is so much emphasis in the schools today on testing that our kids are used to a culture where there is always a right answer. Every school district wants to show that they are doing their job so they test kids frequently. So much time is spent teaching to the test and not actually helping kids learn how to independently process information. When you ask them a question they try to figure out what answer you want to hear. Many times I had to tell kids "I honestly want to know what you think. There is no right or wrong answer." Kids are afraid to answer because they might be wrong. Consequently this affects their thought process on the floor or field, so coaches have to spend time teaching their players the skill of adjusting to change. That's why it's so important to get kids on your team that eat, sleep and breathe the game. They learn by watching or by playing pickup ball where it isn't always structured and they have to figure out how to be successful.

Parents Pushing Their Kids Too Much. As I mentioned before, college is very expensive so parents put a lot of effort into their kids' athletic development. They figure if they spend money now getting their kid coached/trained, then it will lead to a scholarship. I understand that thought process. But I've been at games when parents were yelling at their kids to run faster and jump higher. When I hear that I'm thinking "*You* gave that kid her genes. So if you can't run fast and jump high, how can you expect her to?" Just let the kid enjoy the game. There are so many ways to earn a living with a career in sports without touching a ball.

Competition vs. Collaboration. Coaches at the youth level spend a lot of time teaching kids about competition. And while that is important, not enough time is spent on the concepts of collaboration and teamwork. Working with others to achieve a common goal is an important skill for leaders. There are many ways to teach this part of leadership but sports has a unique way of helping young people grasp the concept of building alliances. Athletics is a living laboratory; an incubator where kids develop collaborative skills. The constant exposure to challenges helps kids understand the importance of partnerships. They learn to be selfless and that they have to be willing to give of themselves for the greater good.

A Sense of Entitlement. 21st century kids expect to be handed everything by the time they get to college coaches because it has always been that way for them. They have always asked for and gotten a cell phone, video games, gear, and most importantly praise (whether they deserve it or not). They have a hard time understanding "no." One time I bought my players some really nice fleece warm-ups that they requested. I have always been a coach who stresses making academics a priority, so I told them if their grades were good at midterm, then I would give them the suits. Well, only half the kids had good grades so I only gave the team the top half of their suits. They weren't happy but I explained to them that in the real world, if you don't produce you don't get rewarded. Sometimes that feeling of entitlement extends to how they are coached. If they don't like the way they are being coached it's the coach's fault for their lack of performance. And while I admit we could all do a better job at coaching, the words of one of my former coaches comes to mind. "I have forgotten more basketball than you will ever know".

Mixed/Bad Messages from Society. We see so many bad examples of how to act in the news today. Kids see a lack of accountability and leaders who don't think that rules apply to them. Look no further than our political process and you will see what I mean. Kids get bombarded with mixed messages constantly so it's no wonder they don't understand how to achieve and sustain success.

With all I have discussed in this chapter you need to decide if you want to be a head coach or remain an assistant because each has a different role with the players. Given that 21st century kids require a lot more positive reinforcement, what are you capable of? I personally struggle with that concept. I'm from the old school where you do things the right way because you are supposed to and not always for an immediate reward. I constantly have to work to be less critical of players and give them more pats on the back. It's something I know I have to keep getting better at and I try to do that by giving them what I call PEDS. PEDS stands for Positive Emotional Deposits. It's similar to a bank. I try to remember to give them genuine positive reinforcement consistently on and off the court so that when I do have to "coach" them they understand it is because I care and want them to be successful. Then hopefully they will understand I am helping and not having them do things because I enjoy making their lives miserable. But it isn't always easy. I know there are times when I should spend more time pointing out the positives instead of dwelling on the negatives.

I would be remiss if I didn't say that I do actually envy some of the skill sets 21st century kids have. There is real value in their ability to multitask and compartmentalize and sometimes we should be more open to the way they do things. For example, when I first started requiring my players to attend study hall I would not let them wear ear buds. When I studied I needed a quiet room to get things done. But after I thought about it I decided they should not have to do everything the way I did. I just wanted them to get good grades. So I allowed the ear buds for a while as an experiment. At the end of the semester their grades were fine so I stopped fighting it.

I think it's important for coaches to recognize that most kids today are still good kids, regardless of the different way they are being raised. They still want to please their coaches and they still want to do well. The 21st century kid will still run through a wall, but now there has to be an explanation and maybe, just maybe they will do it; if they think about it…if it makes sense…if it doesn't hurt…if their friend will do it with him or her...if they have time...if it doesn't go over the NCAA mandated hours...if it's going to result in immediate playing time...

Chapter 6
ARE WE THERE YET?

How long does it take for a message to get through to an 18-22 year old? Do you have to tell them something 10, 20, 50 times before they grasp the importance of the message? This is the challenge all coaches (and I suspect parents and teachers as well) face on a daily basis. Intellectually we coaches understand that maturity is a process that takes time; that each person develops at his or her own pace. But in athletics there are so many external factors that make us wish the process could be both shortened and coordinated amongst our players. And we hope it can be done before our contracts are up.

So how does one deal with navigating the different maturity levels of his or her players? One way is to know your filters as a coach. We all see things through different lenses. By that I mean we have different life experiences that shape how we do things. It's only natural that when we are dealing with players we reference those experiences. I feel I am fairly aware of most of my filters but I'm sure there are some things I just don't think about. How about you? Have you ever considered what factors contribute to the decisions you make when interacting with your players? People in general have many filters, whether or not they are aware of them. I am only going to address the ones I think coaches deal with the most; culture, family, gender, and economics.

    Culture is probably the broadest term because it encompasses so many areas. When you use that word you could be speaking of race, ethnicity, geography, or age. People are hesitant to speak of race or ethnicity because they are afraid it will create negative conversation. But I believe it's important because it still permeates every facet of our society so it naturally will be part of the conversation in athletics. One of the wonderful aspects of athletics is that it brings all kinds of people together. And although there is still much work to be done with regards to diversity and inclusion in athletics (and in our country), sports help us celebrate our similarities rather than focusing on our differences. Be sure your staff is diverse. This is important because we live in a global economy in the 21st century and the one color that matters most is green (as in $). Culture — especially race and ethnicity, contributes greatly to a person's early "psychic scripting." Each subculture places greater emphasis on differing values — whether it's money, education, family, religion or ethics. If your kids aren't prepared to interact successfully with people who didn't grow up like them, don't look like, talk like, or act like them, then they aren't going to be successful. I always joke with my players that if I don't help them in that area then they'll never make any money and won't be able to donate to the program. But if you really think about it, that's true.

Having awareness of a kid's family situation is extremely important. Not every family operates the same way. What your family considers important in life isn't necessarily the same for the kids you coach. Many families have dysfunction, but you may deal with some kids for whom total dysfunction is a way of life. Some families value education, some do not. You could have a kid on your team who has been told it is okay not to go to school if they don't feel like it. Or worse, you may be recruiting a kid who can't go to school because they need to work to help support their family. Some families have parents who feel it's more important to be a friend to their kids because they are not equipped with the skills necessary to parent effectively. They want their child to like them to avoid confrontation. I paid a lot of attention to how kids treated their caregivers when I made home visits. If a kid disrespected her parents she was not someone I wanted to coach. I knew I was not going to tolerate that or allow her to disrespect me, her peers or others at my institution. None of this means you shouldn't try to help kids. But if you choose to coach kids who have issues, you and the people at your institution had better be equipped to help them.

Age is something we don't think about often but it clearly affected my experience coaching. One day I was in a meeting with my players when I realized I was 25 years older than my freshman. That's a very wide gap of life experience. Knowing that, is it fair to expect her to be fully mature at that time in her life? The players' maturity level is nowhere near ours as adults. The challenge we coaches face is to have empathy and understanding for our youngsters' issues without lowering our expectations of them. That's hard to do because we see things from an older, wiser point of view. Twenty-five years is a long time to go through life's challenges, triumphs, and failures while gaining wisdom. But there are certain things that stand the test of time and we should always emphasize them. Respect for others, hard work, and treating others the way we want to be treated will never change, regardless of the decade, century, or age of the individual.

Gender is always a touchy subject but it's important; especially for male coaches. It's no secret that men see some things differently than women and we should acknowledge the different processes. I have worked with both genders and while the x's and o's are the same I recognize that girls and boys don't grow up the same way. They are socialized differently from birth. Male coaches of women need to recognize this and make sure they have women on their staffs to address situations and issues they may not be familiar with. Having said that, I think men coaching women should still have the same expectations of their players, regardless of gender.

I can't discuss gender without mentioning that the number of female head coaches has dwindled in the last few years and that is a trend we *must* work to reverse. In 1972 Congress passed Title IX, a law making it illegal to discriminate on the basis of sex under any program receiving federal assistance. This law applies to all educational programs, including athletics. An unexpected outcome of Title IX is that coaching women's sports has become lucrative enough to support an entire family. Therefore, many men have entered the profession, decreasing the overall number of female head coaches. In 2017 there are many young women who have played their entire career for a male head coach. It is crucial that we increase the number of female head coaches at all levels for several reasons. It's essential for the young women we coach to understand that they too can be leaders. They must see people who look like them as head coaches or top administrators in order to aspire to the profession. I'm concerned that visual is dwindling. Something else people don't think about often enough is that our young men need to be educated that women are capable leaders. We need more female coaches at the youth level because that is where boys start to form their opinions on what is possible and "normal" in regards to leadership. If they are coached by women then they will understand that we have value and the ability to lead. And if men can coach women's teams, why aren't there more women coaching men's teams? The x's and the o's are the same.

The issue of sexual orientation should also be considered. Our society has made great strides in regards to how we view this issue. Whether you coach men or women, you will have kids on your team who may identify as something other than heterosexual. I never asked any kid I coached about their sexual orientation for two reasons. One, it's none of my business unless they choose to share it with me. Two, it has nothing to do with their performance in the classroom or on the court.

You also have to consider the expectations for your staff. Hopefully we all aspire to be accepting of other people's choices, but what does that mean for you as the leader of the program? How does that inform your hiring process? What kind of example do you set for your players? What message do you send with your actions? To be sure this is a subject that requires much more coverage than a simple paragraph. My goal is simply to help you think about the subject in a broader context.

The final filter is economic. Let's face it; some kids come from money and others don't. Some are well read, some aren't. Some have a great educational foundation and some don't. Coaches also come from different backgrounds. We don't all come from money. I'm a perfect example. Ever since I lost both my parents as a teenager I have had to work for and earn everything I've gotten in life. So I have a really difficult time with any kid who is on full scholarship and doesn't work hard. I recognize that about myself and work very hard not to expect kids to think the same way I do because they haven't gone through what I have. But that doesn't change my expectation that they hold up their end of the bargain; the school provides you with an education and you only have to do two things; make academics a priority and work to become the best player you can be.

Is our desire for our kids to be mature realistic? In my opinion a coach's job is not to dwell on where a kid is in the maturity process, but rather to believe in what the kid has the ability to become. Coaches should be aware of our filters and

> "...a coach's job is not to dwell on where a kid is in the maturity process, but rather to believe in what the kid has the ability to become."

understand that our approaches to kids might need to be different. However, our *expectations* for them should not be. Having the expectation of sustained excellence is not only reasonable, it should be demanded. Besides, coaches and players want the same thing–to win games. The coach's job is to help his or her players connect the dots between what they say they want and what it will take for them to achieve it. In doing so, we coaches may actually grow ourselves.

Chapter 7

AND THE WINNER IS...

Recruiting is the lifeblood of every program. You're a great coach if you have great players; not so great if you don't. With that in mind, developing recruiting skills is an essential part of becoming a successful coach. Acquiring players has changed so much over the years. When I started coaching my boss just told me to go to a game, watch the game, then talk to the players. She didn't tell me what to say or how to say it. Predictably I wasn't very successful in the beginning. Now there are tons of vehicles to educate yourself that include the traditional seminars and books, in person seminars, webinars, and other software. But the basic premise of selling your program is pretty much the same. Even with all the technological advances it's still about relationships. It's still about making a kid feel on top of the world. Coaches spend a lot of time making each kid feel special, talking about and showing them how their unique

> "Recruiting requires hard work, consistency, and attention to detail. The best and most successful recruiters are simply the hardest, most efficient workers."

skills will help elevate a program. Recruiting requires hard work, consistency, and attention to detail. The best and most successful recruiters are simply the hardest, most efficient workers. It's not rocket science. With that in mind there are a few factors I consider vital in the recruiting process for all coaches:

Never Work at a Place or for a Coach You Don't Believe In. If you have good core values it would be hard to lie about your head coach. 21st century kids are smart and will see right through you anyway. For example, if you tell them your coach believes in academics but the program's published Academic Progress Rate is below the minimum, they will wonder what else you aren't telling the truth about. With the Internet and other types of social media everything is out in the open. If you make statements about your coach, kids will simply seek confirmation. They can Google anything and contact current and former players via social media to verify information within seconds. Don't lie to them and lose your credibility.

Know the Mission of Your Institution. It's important you are familiar with the mission statements of your university and your athletic department. Sports are often the "front porch" of the university. Coaches are an extension of the university's admissions office. Many times a person's first introduction to your school is through their experience with its teams. You need to know the mission for several reasons. One, your messaging should be consistent with the university's when you represent the school. You don't want to be promoting something that isn't true. Second, the mission will determine what kind of student-athlete you recruit. A good example of this is when I was working at the Naval Academy. When I recruited post players I would have loved to get kids who were big and strong, held their ground, and could clear space for rebounds. But I couldn't recruit those kids because they would never have been able to complete the obstacle course and all the other physical training that was part of their curriculum. I also had to recruit kids with certain personalities. They had to be thick skinned, mature, and goal oriented because they served five years in the Navy after graduation. You don't ever want to recruit a kid that doesn't "fit" what your university's mission is. Finally, you need to be sure the mission aligns with your core values. If not, you won't be happy working there.

Always Be Honest. If you're honest you don't have to remember what you said. The truth is consistent. It doesn't change and it stands the test of time. If you're ever involved in an NCAA investigation make sure you tell the truth. It's not worth risking your career. When I was little I remember my mother telling me to "fess up" when asked if I did something wrong. She said if I told the truth the whuppin' I was going to get anyway would be much less severe than if I lied. I always think of that when I make decisions.

Stick To Your Principles. Follow the rules. If someone asks you to change your core values then you don't want to work for him or her. No one is perfect and coaches make mistakes. There are so many rules in the NCAA manual it's impossible to know them all. Even the ones we profess to know by passing the recruiting test every year are confusing. But we're all old enough to know right from wrong. If you have to cheat, then it's time to leave. *Nothing* is worth losing your reputation and integrity over. The fact remains that there are rules to abide by but it's difficult to legislate ethics.

Be Professional. The best recruiters are serious about and efficient with their work. They know when they need to come early to the gym and when to stay late. You do need to take care of yourself, but there's a way to accomplish that and still get the job done. Organization and efficiency are the keys. Do your research. Know what your head coach wants or what your program needs. During recruiting _do your job_. Don't spend all your time talking, joking around with other coaches because you never know who is watching. Head coaches keep a file in the back of their minds for future reference. You could blow an opportunity at a job and not even know it.

Have the Recruit's Best Interest at Heart. You would be doing that if they say yes to you anyway. I would tell kids to visit other schools if they weren't sure about coming to play for me. I told them that because I was confident in what I had to offer and if they decided to come to my school they wouldn't think "coulda, shoulda, woulda". I wanted them to make an informed decision and be sure, because if a kid doesn't feel good about his or her choice it's counterproductive for both parties. They lose a year when they decide to transfer and you are short one player that you invested time in and energy on.

Recruit Kids with Good Character. Be sure the kids you recruit know right from wrong. What does that mean? First, let's make sure we aren't being judgmental or stereotyping kids because the definition of "family" is not so cut and dry in the 21st century. There are many different kinds of support systems. Some kids live with two parents; some come from single-parent homes. Some live with grandparents, legal guardians, and sometimes even their coach. Just make sure the kid is being supported by a caregiver who helps him or her understand right from wrong. Do your research and communicate with everyone who is associated with that student-athlete.

Recruiting Is Cyclical. Sometimes the upcoming class in your local area is outstanding and sometimes it just isn't very good. Be sure to expand your recruiting contacts to various geographical areas to get you through the lean years. Plan at least two classes ahead so you're not scrambling when signing period arrives. You always need a backup plan because players have backup schools. Don't get caught up in time spans for recruiting. You can recruit a kid for two years, lose him or her, then talk to someone for only two weeks and get a commitment immediately. When I was a head coach I had managed the recruiting process to the point where we could offer juniors a scholarship so they would know we were committed to saving them a spot on our roster when they graduated high school. I was really excited because my staff and I had worked hard to get the local community and AAU teams familiar with our program. One year I extended an early offer to two kids who happened to be the best players in the area, and when they accepted we were elated. Soon after the offer we asked them for their academic information. They kept making excuses for missing the dates of the SAT. I should have recognized the red flags but I ignored them because I was so happy to have two players coming that would have an immediate impact on our program. The delays lasted through summer recruiting. Finally in September I realized that there was a reason they didn't want me to see their grades; their academic records were not very good. So I had two issues to deal with; I had to rescind the offer when I ultimately received their transcripts and I had to start recruiting again after heavily pursuing only those two kids for two years. We scrambled, but in the span of two weeks in October we reconnected with two other kids, had them on a campus visit, they committed, and signed in November. I felt bad about rescinding the offers but realized that we should have done our homework before offering them the opportunity. As it turned out, the two kids we ended up signing were in many ways much better suited for the program. Remember, the only constant about recruiting is that it changes on a daily basis.

Do Not Negative Recruit. Bashing other programs will only come back to haunt you. Kids actually don't like it when you do that and it doesn't speak well about you or your program. Spend your time telling kids what's great about your program and nothing else.

Be Gracious in Defeat. When a kid tells you "no", don't waste too much energy on the experience. Evaluate if you could have done something better and move on. Sometimes you will hear no more than yes if you're not a top program. But even the most elite programs in the country get told no once in awhile. Wish the kid well in his or her future endeavors when s/he turns you down. Never "go off" on a prospect. In the future they might be unhappy, want to transfer and you want your school to be the first one on their minds at that time.

In the end none of us gets every recruit we want. But if you work hard and do it the right way you will get what you need. Stay diligent, stay confident, and stay true to your principles.

Chapter 8

WOMAN/MAN IN THE MIRROR

How much do you think your kids pay attention to the way you conduct yourself? Do you think they are really watching what you say and do? We think our kids don't listen to us because we repeat things so often. I have always been fine with repeating things a couple of times to my kids because I give them the benefit of the doubt that my voice doesn't carry or they just "weren't with me" at a particular moment. But it grinds on my nerves when I repeat something three, four, five times to one kid, then another one either asks the same question five minutes later or makes the very same mistake I corrected their teammate for. This happens to every coach on every level because kids are in their own world most of the time. But whether we realize it or not our kids are listening to us (albeit selectively). And they are *always* watching us; both what we say and what we do. I read the following story (the author is unknown) from John Wooden's book *One On One*. It is a perfect illustration of how we interact with others - and that can either be a good or a bad example to our players.

A seminary student was taking his last final exam. The final question was worth 50% of his grade. "What is the name of the dorm custodian?" The young man was enraged and confronted his professor. The professor looked up and spoke gently, "Jesus showed compassion for, and interest in, those who occupied the lower stations in life. If you are going to represent Jesus properly, the custodian is the first person you should have met. For four years, she has cleaned your room, scrubbed your toilet and emptied your trash. You have had four years to learn her name. Until she becomes of interest to you as a person, you don't qualify to become a pastor."

Think about how you treat people on a daily basis. Do you know the names of your custodial and facilities staff? Do you know anything about them other than that they take care of your building? Do you scowl and not say hello to people the day after your team loses a game? It's important to develop genuine relationships with your co-workers because they will be a part of your success (or failure). Be an example to your players and treat people appropriately. Be a good teammate.

Kids are so smart in the 21st century that they can't wait to tell you if you aren't living up to the same standards you require of them. I have always thought that as a coach I should model the behavior I expect of my players. My goal has always been to try to conduct myself in such a manner that I would not be a hypocrite. I remember when I was in high school my coach would always yell at us to run faster because she thought we were being lazy. Mind you, she never worked out herself so that really made me mad. I thought then that if I was ever in charge of a group of people I wouldn't ask them to do something I wasn't willing to do myself. So if I ask my kids to do preseason workouts at 6:00 A.M., I am there with them. I may be doing the "old lady" workout, but they see I am as committed to strength and conditioning as I expect them to be.

One of John Wooden's best quotes is "A leader's most powerful ally is his or her own example". That means coaches should live the example of what we want our kids to be. There are several areas where this concept is important. First, it's important that you don't try to be perfect. It's okay to admit when you make mistakes (by mistakes I'm not condoning blatant rules violations or extreme lack of judgment). Kids need to see examples of redemption and resilience in their coaches. If not, then they will try to be perfect and that is counterproductive for both you and them. Showing vulnerability has always been hard for me because I thought that if I only showed my kids strength then they would be strong too. I only shared emotion, caring, and concern behind closed doors. And I didn't tell my kids collectively that I loved them until my fourth year as a head coach. Outside of my office I was always the pillar of strength because I thought that's what my team needed. But it turns out it was good for them to see me sometimes when I wasn't at my best or strongest, and that this didn't undermine my authority as leader of the program. In fact, they *and* I benefited from seeing my humanity.

Sometimes it's good for your kids to laugh at your expense. Once during a particularly rough period in the season I could tell my kids didn't want to hear my same old speech. So instead of starting practice by watching film I decided to show them pictures and articles of me from my playing days in college. Every once in awhile I pull them out to remind myself that I actually was an athlete who could run up and down the court more than just a couple of times before getting winded or hurt. After they picked themselves up off the floor from laughing at the short shorts we used to wear back in the day, we had a pretty good practice.

Another fun thing I did was to have all the kids write an essay on why they loved basketball. At the time we weren't winning many games and I thought we needed to go back to the beginning and remember why we started to play in the first place. I had the coaches (including myself) write one as well. We all shared our essays out loud and then I had them copied and bound in a book for each person. It's a keepsake they will always have and it reminded them when basketball got rough that *it is just a game* and we should simply enjoy that we get to play it whenever we want.

An important area coaches should be concerned about is their perception in public. I know a lot of young coaches think, "Why do I have to hide who I am just because I coach?" I don't want to give the

> "Once you become part of an organization everything you do (good or bad) affects the people in that organization."

impression that coaches have to be on the DL (down low) about their personal lives. Your personal life is just that--personal. However, when you coach you have a responsibility to represent your program, department, and institution in an appropriate manner.

I always reminded my kids not to act or think in a vacuum. Once you become part of an organization everything you do (good or bad) affects the people in that organization. Don't go out to bars, get wasted, and post pictures on social media or tweet something you will regret later because it could create negative consequences for your program and for you. In the 21st century age of instant media coaches have to be careful with what we do and say because it will remain on the Internet in perpetuity. You don't have to walk on eggshells and none of us are perfect. But we are old enough not to be stupid and to learn from our mistakes. Be observant and use other people's mistakes as teachable moments. No one is immune to negative consequences. Witness the recent scandals at some of our most respected colleges and universities. These incidents bring down the respect of our entire profession—as well as our colleagues across the campuses. Coaching is a public trust. Parents are placing their children in our hands. We owe it to them to earn that respect every day. Do your best to be what you are asking your kids to be; honest, genuine, and hardworking. It's great to learn from your mistakes; it's a lot easier to learn from someone else's. Try to do the right thing.

Chapter 9
BE WHO WE BE

"Be who we be. If we be who we ain't, we ain't who we be". I gave this quote to my kids on one of our game day scout sheets. When I asked if they had ever heard this of course I got blank stares. One kid asked me if I found it on the web. I reminded her that in the "old days" people actually passed down information by mouth. She was perplexed. I then asked if they knew what it meant. As prophetic as this statement is I was not surprised that kids who aren't fully mature emotionally didn't pick up on what I was trying to convey.

What I wanted them to understand was that if we expect to be successful and reach the goals we set for ourselves, we would need to consistently be at our best with what we decided was our identity. We needed to do the right things to the best of our ability as often as possible. So I asked them "Who are we?" Again there was no answer. I finally had to remind them that who we are is the team that beat the #1 team in the country on their home court. Who we are is a team that has consistently pushed ranked teams to their limit at home and away. As weird as it seems you may actually have to remind your kids how great they are and of the wonderful things they have accomplished. A lot of coaches don't do that often enough.

If you think about it, asking a team "Who are we?" is a hard question to answer when the kids probably don't yet know who they are as individuals. I would venture to say that none of us knew exactly who we were from ages 18-22. We thought we knew more than we actually did about how the world works and we certainly didn't spend a lot of time thinking about who we were individually.

Consistency is a common hurdle teams strive to get over as they compete at the highest level. Coaches talk about it every day, every practice, and every game. Sometimes it sinks in and sometimes it doesn't. The biggest challenge coaching staffs have is helping their teams understand that they have to "connect the dots" between what they say they want and executing to actually achieve those goals, especially when you initially take over a program. We try to be examples in our daily communication and relationships with our teams and hope they process that interaction. But we sound like a broken record when we repeat the same things over and over and over and over again. It is extremely frustrating for a coach when you feel like you haven't been heard.

I like to compare the process of consistency to the mile run. Each of the four laps in that race is totally different. The first lap you're off to the races. You have high expectations for your performance. You're in the big chair and have all these great ideas now that you are in charge. Everything is new and you have a lot of energy and plenty of ideas. You are full of hope and the world is your oyster.

The second lap is the first opportunity you have to monitor your progress. You evaluate your start and wonder if you are running at the right pace. Am I doing the right things to be successful (signing the right kids for my system, gaining the trust of the kids I inherited, giving my kids the correct workouts so the team can get better, winning the games we should win)? If you're behind you need to speed up. If you're ahead you need to keep a steady pace.

The third lap is the hardest because you know there is an end to the race but you hurt so much you really can't think about it. Even if you are doing the right things you know it's going to take time to see any results. Lots of unforeseen obstacles crop up that can distract you from your mission. You lose a key player to injury or academics and that messes with your depth. Or you win some games you shouldn't and lose some that you should have won.

I experienced this in a big way one year. We were scheduled to play the #1 program in the country on their campus and I was stressed out the day before. The kids weren't focused and I didn't think we were practicing well. After only a few minutes I threw them out of the gym because I didn't think they were serious enough about the opportunity we had to move the program forward. I didn't sleep that night because I realized that they were just kids and they hadn't thought that far ahead. I thought "Crap. I just threw my team out of practice the day before we play the #1 team in the country and we are going to get our heads handed to us!" But you know what? I underestimated my kids. They went up there with all the confidence in the world and pulled it off. All I said to the team before the game was "For us to win this game, each one of you has to do something you have never done before to help us be successful". And that's what they did. Go figure!

After the game everyone was elated. When we got into the locker room they were bouncing off the walls crazy with joy. I walked in acting real cool with a straight face and told them to calm down; to act like we were supposed to win. They continued to go nuts and I acted like it was no big deal and told them to sit down. They were bursting at the seams and couldn't understand it. Why was I not as happy and excited as they were? After they sat down I let a few seconds go by with a really stern look on my face, but then I couldn't keep up the charade. I burst into a big smile, started jumping up and down and screamed "We just beat the #1 team in the country!" I will never forget the happy looks on their faces when they started screaming again.

The kids were like rock stars the next day at school because they accomplished something no team in any sport there had ever done. We were all on cloud nine. I tried my best to keep them from being overconfident for the next game three days later, but it didn't work. In retrospect I probably should have given them the next day off from practice except for some shooting and we should have just watched film. I think they were so tired and emotionally spent from the big win that they didn't have anything in the tank for the next game. We actually lost to the last place team in the league. See what I mean by obstacles? Sometimes the obstacle can be the progress you make. How does your team handle prosperity? How do you as their coach handle it? The third lap is a crucial time where the coach needs to stay focused so that s/he can help the kids with consistency. Don't let the setbacks keep you from achieving your goal.

On the final lap you can see the finish line tape. Finally there are some tangible results for your efforts. You

> "Sometimes the obstacle can be the progress you make. How does your team handle prosperity? How do you as their coach handle it?"

win more games than you lose, recruits start contacting you first, and people start complimenting you on your team's performance. All of a sudden "you know how to coach" and people don't second guess you as much. You can take a deep breath because you know you have the ability to "finish". There's still much work to be done, but at least you can see success on the horizon. It's a good feeling.

    I think consistency is the hardest concept for teams to embrace. Every program at every level struggles with it and it can be very frustrating. But every once in a while your kids *do* hear, they *do* perform and are successful. And when that light bulb turns on for them and they are so excited and happy, it brings a lot of joy to coaches. We wish only that our players learn to "be who we be" before they leave us and are able to apply it to their daily lives. If we can help them do that then we have done our jobs. Selfishly we know it may translate to success for our programs as well.

Chapter 10
IF MAMA AIN'T HAPPY...

This is an old saying that still rings true in the 21st century. It means that if the family matriarch isn't doing well (literally and figuratively speaking) then the entire household is off balance. One of the hardest things to do in coaching is to find a sense of balance in your life. Like mothers, coaches (men and women) spend so much time tending to the needs of others (players, significant others, assistants, etc) that we often forget a really important person (ourselves). And while that may sound selfish it's really quite logical. If we don't take care of ourselves, we will be no good to others. There's a basketball analogy I like that Russell Simmons uses in his book *SuperRich–A Guide to Having It All*. He says "...basketball coaches always stress having a strong inside-out game...if their team can first establish its inside game...then it will have a much easier time with its outside game...when you work on becoming strong on the inside first, that success will open up the rest of your game." Basically he's saying that you need to get your own house in order so that you will truly be free to positively impact others. We lose ourselves so often because we have a servant leadership mentality and are immersed in our programs; whether it's pushing kids to reach their full potential, or dealing with external entities like administrators, donors, parents, and alums. Even the simplest things slip our minds. When I first started in the business, I was very aware from observing coaches that I didn't want to cheat myself (and those around me) of a positive experience. I learned early what not to do and I made a promise to myself never to forgo good (decent?) nutrition, exercise, etc. so that I would always be balanced.

Nutrition is often the first thing to go. On my first day in the office as a head coach I worked about fourteen hours and didn't realize I had not eaten all day. For a period of time, I had to set my cell phone alarm to remember to feed myself. When we're on the road recruiting there are so many games to see we do one of two things–we eat junk or we don't eat at all. We all know it's bad but the eagerness to be successful in recruiting overrides our common sense. Or we drown our sorrows late at night in food because we lose a game. Somehow a McDonald's quarter pounder meal (with two apple pies for a dollar!) tastes really good and makes us feel better after yelling at some kids who have been given a complete scouting report, yet still somehow won't keep a post player from turning to his or her right shoulder and making the only move he or she has!

Try to eat right. If you can afford a chef hire one. If not, try cooking all your meals for the week on your day off. Freeze them and microwave each meal when you are ready to eat. Either that or bribe your significant other to cook for you! And when you are on the road go to the grocery store and buy healthy snacks with your meal money. That will keep you from going hungry until you have time to eat a decent meal. I also try to only drink water or unsweetened tea while I am on the road so I stay hydrated.

Exercise is the next thing to go. I still have the six-pack abs I had in college; only now they are under a layer of fat. Coaches work so hard and so long we rationalize that when we get home we're tired and will get up tomorrow and work out. We know when our heads hit the pillow there's no way we are going to wake up before we have to, but it sounds good anyway. And exercise is the last thing on our minds when our backs hurt because we were stupid enough to guard the biggest post player on our team while trying to show our kids how to play post defense--or show an offensive lineman how to protect his quarterback. But you know what? I solved a lot of problems when I worked out. Somehow I was able to focus more on what was bothering me and work out a solution. Find an exercise you like and make an effort to stay committed to working out at least three days a week.

A key part of balance is making sure we know who we are away from our sport. So many others define us only as coaches and we get trapped in that mindset as well. I always tell my players to find out who they are outside of athletics because *some day it will end*. And if you haven't developed a well-rounded life you will be miserable when your sport is taken away (voluntarily or involuntarily). Find a hobby away from the game. I'm a big movie buff. Sitting in that cushioned chair for a couple of hours is a great way for me to release stress. Also, after the end of every season I always take a class. I do it for three reasons--to keep my brain from turning to mush, to meet new people who have nothing to do with athletics or the institution where I work, and again to visibly show my love of learning to my players. The classes help me get away from the game, reset, recharge, and appreciate basketball when I return.

> "A key part of balance is making sure we know who we are away from our sport."

Managing your stress level is definitely important for balance. Everyone knows how to coach your team better than you do. They have the benefit of watching the replay and telling you what you should have done or which kid you should have played. You need to have thick skin in our profession because everyone always has an opinion. I received two negative emails from the mother of a kid during my first two years as a head coach. She was mad I didn't play her kid even though we were losing. What she didn't realize is that her kid was a walking turnover. And the email she sent the second year was *after* her kid had already graduated! She proceeded to let me know just how awful a coach I was and how much pleasure she took in watching us lose games. The first thing I thought when I received the emails is "get a life". Then, when I looked at the times she sent the emails (one at 11:30 P.M., the other at 1:30 A.M.) I thought "How sad must your life be that you were thinking of me and wrote those emails at that time of night (morning)?" I felt sorry for her. But in coaching there are people like that who have no life and you are a convenient target for them.

    To stay balanced I keep an envelope near my office desk labeled "Yes, you are doing the right thing". It's full of letters and cards from parents and kids who have written to thank me for what I did for them. When things get really heavy I read these and know that "I done good". And when I get a case of the "big head" and think I'm all that after a big win I remember those emails to bring myself back to earth.

    When you are on the road for games or recruiting things happen that will delay your travel or screw up your schedule. Try to be proactive to minimize these events. The small things make a difference. When you fly, take direct flights. Or if you can't avoid connections, try to route your trips through hubs that don't affect the rest of the country when flights are cancelled (Chicago and Atlanta are examples of this). Leave plenty of time between your flights to get a meal in case you have to go straight to your destination when you land. And it's best to take the first flight out in the morning because the later in the day you wait, the delays get even worse. Have breakfast in a calm, quiet environment. If you start off stressed the rest of your day will go that way too. Finally, find a few minutes a day to just be still and quiet. I call this my "sit and be" time. If you don't trust yourself during recruiting then add it to your daily game schedule.

It is important to realize that your relationship with your players can be negatively affected by your stress level. Whether or not you realize it, how you handle the different stressors in your life plays a huge part in how you coach them. When I don't do a great job of dealing with my stress, I become impatient and easily frustrated at the smallest things. It becomes increasingly difficult for me to communicate with the kids and give them confidence. When a coach is stressed s/he loses what is called "situational awareness". By that I mean we can't or don't see the cumulative negative effect of lack of patience, personal attention, and other important aspects of mentoring and grooming young people. We get so wrapped up in dealing with a particular situation we lose sight of what our purpose is in coaching. As a result, we don't demonstrate the proper concern for our players. Sometimes it's the things our players *don't* say in conversation that are most important. If we are stressed and not actively listening, we don't pick up on those important cues that tell us what a kid is experiencing.

One good way to avoid losing situational awareness is to find an activity and be coached yourself. When you are the "student" you get an entirely different perspective of coaching. You realize how important it is to be positive and to communicate effectively. Some of us have not had a coach since college and forget what that experience is like. Being coached helps you reset your priorities and refocus on what your job is with your players.

After I lost my head coaching job I had the opportunity to reflect on my actions that last season. It wasn't until then that I realized that not dealing adequately with my stress kept me from helping my kids achieve what they were capable of. I just could not get them to reach their full potential because my mind was not clear and at peace with my situation.

I do several things to help manage my stress. First, I never go in the office before I have done something positive for myself--unless I absolutely have to. (If that happens I try to find some other time during the day to get a workout in). I work out as many mornings as I can. I also spend quiet time before I go to work. Sometimes it's only five or ten minutes, but I make sure and get it in every day. To me, taking care of your spirituality is extremely important because it keeps you centered. I also use acupuncture and yoga to keep my karma on an even keel. And I continue to take a nap on the day of a game like I did when I played in college because it helps keep me calm. Find what works for you and stick to a regular schedule.

Remember not to neglect your family. Married or single, children or not, the worst thing you can do is forsake your family for a game. They are the only ones who love you for you and don't want anything but your love and attention. They didn't throw an interception, serve the ball into the net, miss a lay-up, throw a fat pitch that the opponent hit over the fence, or make a bad call. Win or lose your family is always there for you. This is especially important when you are on the road. Use technology to your advantage. With Smartphones, laptops, and IPads there is no excuse for not reminding them every day that you are thinking of them. Use your family as a source to get re-centered when things aren't going well. Richard Barron was always a good example of this for me when I was at Princeton. When his twins were newborns he would always bring one into the meeting room after games so that he wouldn't yell at the players. I always thought it was great when itty-bitty teams were scheduled to come into the locker room after games. It made me watch my tone of voice and what I said because I knew they would be waiting outside the door for us to finish. And moms are the best people in the world to talk to after losses. I could go 0-30 in a season and my mother would still think I am the best coach in the world. If I call to tell her we lost she would always say, "Don't worry baby. You did your best. It's not your fault those damn kids won't do what they are told!"

Finally I make sure that I am not defined by what happens at work. Win or lose a game, good or bad practice, I have the most fun job ever. What a blessing that I get paid to coach! And no matter what happens to me I still have a pretty blessed life. I try to remember people all over the world struggle with oppression and poverty and babies still need their diapers changed. It's easy to forget how lucky we are. Try not to lose perspective.

Chapter 11

ARE YOU VISUALLY IMPAIRED?

"Seeing is believing." At least that's the creed some people live by. But what about the reverse "Believing is seeing?" We talk about visualization to our players hoping to help them be successful, yet how many times do we coaches practice that? Most of the time we concentrate so much on helping our players improve that we forget to work on ourselves.

> "The mind can only hold one thought at a time. It can either be positive or negative."

Visualization is a powerful ally that can be used in many areas of our lives. In coaching it can be helpful or hurtful, depending on your frame of mind. I am big on karma and believe that what a person thinks will ultimately become his or her reality. What we want to happen often dictates how we live and what kinds of things and people are drawn to us. There's a quote from James Allen in his book *As a Man Thinketh* where he says, "A person is limited only by the thoughts that he chooses."

The mind is a strong tool and will do whatever it is commanded to do. But consider that the mind can only hold one thought at a time. It can either be positive or negative. If we think negatively that is how we will "react". If we think positively that is how we will "act". Sometimes we coaches don't apply this to our own work. For example, when we tell our players to "close their eyes and see the basketball going through the hoop" we are trying to help them build their confidence by picturing success. Have you ever pictured yourself diagramming a play at the end of a game, having that play work and winning the game? Do you ever see yourself celebrating because you've just defeated your biggest rival, or won a conference championship, or even a national championship? The following story (author unknown) is a great illustration of this principle.

> A rural church in the middle of farming country had a special service to pray for rain. A drought had hit the area hard and the farmers and community were suffering financially and spiritually. Many people came to the service to pray and, as the pastor looked out over the crowd he was encouraged. However, the thing that inspired him most was a little girl sitting in the front pew, holding a bright red umbrella. Everyone had come to pray for rain, but only the little girl believed enough to bring an umbrella.

I use the time I exercise every day to imagine myself in successful scenarios. I create the scenario, speak the dialogue and script the body language. Where is your umbrella?

Believing is seeing. When we transfer that to some of the most basic components of our programs we can see how effective visualization can be. Recruiting is a great example. The kids we recruit can see through deception and insincerity. If you don't believe in or are not excited about your program they will know. But if you go into a home and communicate a clear concise vision that shows you believe in what you want to accomplish, they will see your passion. They will pick up on your positive energy and want to play for you. Another good example of this concept is a coach's performance at the end of a tight game. If we expect our players to perform successfully under pressure they need to know we have confidence in our own ability to help them get the job done. Visualizing composure, our demeanor and body language is important. But you also must work on that in practice. Everyone can be a much better coach in games by combining the two.

Visualization is a fundamental that should be practiced consistently. You must see yourself as a winning coach on a daily basis. As James Allen says, "A man can only rise, conquer, and achieve by lifting up his thoughts."

Take a few minutes every day and picture yourself succeeding at some aspect of the game. This is important because you will encounter obstacles and have to remain mentally tough to help your team through them. When you do face those obstacles remember two things:

1. **You will not taste victory every time.** It's impossible. Failure is an important part of the learning process. It should be viewed as an opportunity to improve and nothing more.

2. **Perseverance is imperative.** We don't always get what we want when we want it. I read a great quotation from the broadcaster Robin Roberts where she said "God's delays are not His denials". Coaches constantly stress to our players to keep working hard and never give up. We should do the same.

Chapter 12
THROW THE BALL TO THE BLUE TEAM!!!

Managing anger and frustration in games and practices is hard for coaches. When I took over my first team I yelled at the officials a lot. Part of the reason I yelled at them so often is that I felt I couldn't yell at my players too much. It would be counterproductive if I yelled at them every time we made a mistake or did something stupid. Besides, that happened so often my first year I would have lost my voice every game. I also knew as a rookie coach I wasn't going to get calls anyway. So I figured I might as well get my point across and make myself feel better. One of my favorite rants to the players was "I'm not going to lower my expectations to your level! You are going to raise yours to mine!" Thinking back it reminds me of Macbeth's soliloquy in Shakespeare's play. He tells a story and it's "Told by an idiot, full of sound and fury, signifying nothing." I suppose I was trying to channel Vince Lombardi and I fancied myself a young Pat Summitt. The difference between myself and those two people was that they won multiple championships. I used to stomp my feet a lot as if that would make my voice louder and it took me two years to finally realize why I had to ice my knees after every game. After a while the players and officials tuned me out. I was like the teacher in the Charlie Brown cartoon whose voice was always muffled. "Wa wa wa wa wa wa".

We've all given those fiery speeches at halftime that your players are happy to remind you about. I charged a quarter every time a kid cursed my first year as a head coach. The reason I did is because I was afraid their mouths would get us a technical and we weren't good enough to be giving any points away. One day my players reminded me about the time I came into a halftime with a twenty dollar bill and told them it was for the speech I was about to give. I honestly don't remember that, but they thought it was hilarious. Another halftime I was so mad I started my speech by banging on the dry erase board. As I was hitting my hand against the board it occurred to me "This is really going to hurt later on. Why was I doing that to myself?" I had to ice my swollen palm after the game.

Kids don't always respond negatively to screaming. There were many times my seniors reminded me that when I yelled they sensed it was done to motivate them. In the beginning (before I realized it was stupid to try to keep up with the kids) I used to chase behind them when we did sprints. I would yell at the top of my lungs about how we were mentally tough and how it was going to help us to be successful and get through adversity. They told me it got them through the conditioning. One day in my office I was talking with my assistant and some players when the kids recalled a time I had disciplined them for not making academics a priority. Several of the players were messing around in study hall and it was the last straw for me because I had been preaching how important it was to hit the books for quite some time. It was about 8:30 P.M and I was on the way home, tired from a meeting where I was raising money to take them to Alaska. I got a call from my assistant telling me the players were not being serious in study hall. I immediately called my captain, told her to have all the kids meet me in the locker room and to bring their sneakers. Later that week I got a phone call from a parent and I thought, "Here it comes." Imagine my shock when she told me her daughter thought that what I had done was good and wished it happened sooner because the team had not been listening and needed to be disciplined.

Times have changed and now people view profanity differently. I'm not advocating profanity laced speeches because as I get older I realize you should be able to get your point across without using curse words. But when I was a young coach it seemed as if that was the only way to get the kids to listen. I think I thought that they would listen to and hear me better if I yelled. Later on I learned that all it did was raise my blood pressure. I matured as a coach, mellowed out and realized I was setting a bad example. I revised my strategy and tried not to scream too often. I learned to be more selective when raising my voice so they would know when I was really mad.

One thing that helped me communicate without screaming was telling stories. Instead of just repeating the same old stuff all the time I would tell them a story or give them one to read. Sometimes they would process it right away and other times I gave them stories I knew they had to spend some time trying to figure out. For example, when we lost to the last place team after that huge win over the #1 team in the country I told my players to Google MC Hammer. I told them to read about him and let me know what similarities there were with his career and our events from the previous week. For those of you not old enough to remember, MC Hammer was one of the most successful rappers in his heyday. He made millions of dollars throughout his career but he eventually lost a lot of it from mismanagement and poor planning. Just like us, he didn't know how to handle prosperity. He wasn't

> "... know how to handle prosperity... be consistent with doing the things that make you successful in the first place."

consistent with doing the things that made him successful in the first place, but I also wanted them to learn about his resilience and how he put his career and life back together. Telling stories is a great way to get your point across. It keeps the kids' attention and can be a very useful tool.

Each year I grew as a coach, realizing that my body language, facial expressions, and tone of voice made a huge difference in how the kids received my communication. It's amazing how powerful nonverbal communication is. I found my team's demeanor often reflected my own. It's such a simple concept that one would think coaches would be more aware of our actions. But in the heat of a game you really have to concentrate to stay calm. I found that when I was calm my team reflected that emotion. I tried not to yell at players if they went off script because I wanted to encourage them to be independent thinkers. I didn't want them to be robots and mindlessly run plays. I wanted them to be structured when they played, but also think about the game and see opportunities to make plays whenever they presented themselves. But that in itself was frustrating because it takes time for each kid to learn when to go off script and for the others on the floor with them to know how to adjust to the change. I bit my tongue and swallowed my whistle a lot because it took my team a couple of years to get to know my system well enough to have independent thoughts. The other thing I really tried not to do was take a kid out of a game right after she made a mistake. I tried to wait one or two plays before making a substitution. That way they don't get a complex and you don't get the "I'm afraid to make a mistake because you take me out" excuse. By the way, it really grinds on my nerves when a kid says I don't have confidence in her. My response to that is "I show confidence in you every July when I sign your scholarship papers." Sound familiar? I wasn't always successful with positive body language but I tried my best.

Another area I had to improve on was timeouts. When I first started coaching I would just scream at my team for 30 seconds. Then one of my players told me it didn't make things better because I never gave them anything to do that would result in positive changes. So I learned to give them constructive criticism. Before I ended the timeout I would try to give them something specific to focus on. And I finally learned to settle down in timeouts (especially 30 second ones because you don't have a lot of time for wasted words). I stopped yelling and the tone of my voice was more conversational. I would say something like "Seriously ladies, did we work hard at practice to play like this?" or "You do know you're supposed to throw the ball to the people in the blue uniforms, right?" I don't know if I was calmer because my team played better or if my team played better because I was calmer. Either way it was better for my blood pressure.

I'm not saying that I was always able to stay calm and offer sage advice to my players. Many times I channeled my mother and spoke through gritted teeth. But I was fortunate enough to realize early in my head coaching career that going crazy in practice or on the sidelines in a game ultimately did not accomplish very much.

Chapter 13
SECOND WIND

What do you do when the middle of your season rolls around and you and your players are bored and tired with the game and with each other? You've been practicing since preseason and still have half your season to finish. That's a tough time of year when things can get stale. Sometimes it's the easiest and simplest changes that can make a difference.

> "Sometimes it's the easiest and simplest changes that can make a difference."

Have Fun. Lightening the mood is tough when you feel like you need to spend time working on plays; especially if you are losing. You feel like fun is not an efficient use of your time. Your players need work on fundamentals; the team needs work on defense and offense. But this would be the most important time for coaches and players to start enjoying the game again. I didn't do enough of that when I was a head coach. I didn't want any music at practice; I didn't want to take away time from my practice schedule. It wasn't until after a few years that I allowed some music and fun stuff to break up the monotony. Sometimes we played dodge ball, ultimate Frisbee, or football in the gym instead of practicing for two hours. The kids especially liked dodge ball because they could fire balls and hit the coaches, and not get in any trouble. I'm old school so that approach was hard for me. But I know my players and assistants appreciated the respite. Do something unexpected and fun for your team once in awhile. Surprise and educate them at the same time. Set up a community service activity so that they know how fortunate they are. Then maybe take them to a cool place for a team dinner. Sometimes I would take my team to the movies and they thought it was the greatest thing in the world that they got to order snacks from the concession stand to eat during the movie.

Cut Your Practice Time Down. If your players don't know your offensive and defensive philosophy by the middle of your season they shouldn't be playing anyway. By then you should only be tweaking what you do a little just to throw in a few surprises. If you're winning you certainly don't want to make too many changes. If you're losing, spending more time in practice is just going to tick your players off and frustrate the coaching staff. Prioritize what you need to do and move on. It's also important to cut practice time because some teams have kids who play a lot of minutes. You don't want them to be worn down as you finish the stretch run in conference play. They need to be as fresh as possible for the postseason and the last thing you want to do is aggravate minor injuries and have them turn into something major. Partly because of facility issues and partly because of fatigue, I used to make my team a promise every February. If we won and had two days before our next game I would only practice one hour the next day. Even if the game was on a Saturday and we had three days between games (one being the required day off mandated by the NCAA) I would keep my promise. It was difficult (because we coaches rarely stick to a practice schedule) but I kept my word every time.

Change Your Drills. We all have our favorite drills. But after a while the players get bored. Don't be stubborn. Change things up. You have enough colleagues that can recommend different approaches. And what difference does it make how your tasks are accomplished if you get the end result you want? Sometimes I would let my kids plan practice. This served two purposes. First, it forced them to see that productive practices actually have to be thought out so they flow seamlessly. Second, they were more likely to be invested in practice if they were doing the drills they like. The only stipulation I had was that I would tell them what we needed to work on. Inevitably they would use drills we already had that they enjoyed. But once in a while they would bring new drills from their high school or AAU days that I actually liked and would keep for the rest of the season. Don't be surprised if you learn some cool, new things from your players.

Bring in Other Voices. Kids tune out the head coach after a while so I would bring in guest speakers toward the end of the season. Sometimes I let other coaches run part of my practice so I could learn something new. It was as much for me as for the players. I got a break and the kids listened better. Most of the time my guests would say things I consistently emphasized, but they had their own unique way of communicating. You would be surprised what kinds of things you can learn from other people. A sample of my guests included a guy from the grounds crew, a Lt. Colonel I coached at the US Naval Academy, an alumna in politics, our men's basketball coach, our compliance director (not to talk about rules; she just loved watching them play), and the supervisor of officials in the NBA. Be eclectic with your choices. They don't always need to have backgrounds in your sport. And don't be stubborn. Yours does not have to be the only voice. It's not about you and your ego. It's about the kids and what's best for the team.

Chapter 14
TEMPERATURE GAUGE

It's important when you get into coaching that you consistently assess the climate of athletics. Coaches just want to coach and we don't want to be bothered with a whole bunch of other stuff. We're competitors. That's our makeup. In our minds, "Why play if you don't want to win?" So much goes into preparing to win games. We scout, recruit, and study film. But if we're not careful we get so busy with our jobs we lose sight of the fact that athletics is a business (at all levels in the 21st century). As such we need to be aware of our environment. For instance, when we look at opportunities we all know to ask about the budgets, salaries, support staff, etc. But we should also look at the infrastructure and leadership of the school. Why? Both can directly affect whether or not you succeed. Ask these questions:

1. How stable is the leadership of the institution and the athletic department. Is there a lot of turnover?

2. Is there a clear, concise strategic plan for the institution that includes the athletic department?

3. Is athletics viewed positively at that institution for the value it can add to the university's mission?

4. Are the proper things in place to help you succeed?
    -Tangible (budget, facilities, marketing, support staff, etc)
    -Intangible (Are there good kids with talent in the program who make academics a priority? Is the AD accessible without needing an appointment? Does the AD come to your games? Does s/he know and talk to student-athletes from all the teams?)

5. Are there people at the institution that look like you in every department? Is the school genuinely committed to diversity (ethnic, geographical, economic, cultural, intellectual, etc)?

6. Do the coaches in the department support one another's programs or is there an "I'm only in it to get mine" mentality with everyone "rowing in their own boat"? If it's the latter that's a reflection of the leadership in the department.

7. Can you be happy living in the area? (If not, you won't be able to convince recruits to come play there.)

8. Are the people that work there happy? Do they enjoy their jobs?

9. Will there be opportunities for you to grow and mature professionally (inside and outside of the department)?

Make sure the AD and the President's positions have a history of stability at your institution. If not, constant policy and philosophical changes can hinder and sometimes impede your progress. That's not to say those positions don't turn over occasionally. But pay attention. If that occurs often don't take the job (or if you realize it afterwards, then you need to plan your exit strategy).

The reality is that as a coach there are many factors beyond your control that have a direct impact on your success. You need to minimize as many of those factors as possible.

Another area you should pay attention to is the climate involving the student-athletes. The NCAA makes student-athlete well-being a priority. They are concerned about making sure the student-athlete has a quality experience. That is as it should be. And I would venture to say that most coaches share the same concern. But consider the type of kid we are coaching in the 21st century and how they have grown up. Remember what I talked about in "I Know, But..."? In return for monetary aid, student-athletes have academic and athletic obligations. During the season the NCAA allows coaches to mandate 20 hours of athletically related activities. Compare a full scholarship to someone who works forty hours in the real world for minimum wage. Let's say your institution costs $40,000 a year and let's say minimum wage is $8/hour. If a person works 40 hours a week for 52 weeks a year they make $16,640 (8 x 40 x 52). And that is before taxes. College coaches can only ask kids for half that amount of time. In this scenario, the student-athlete receives more than someone who puts in twice as much work earns. That is what drives coaches crazy.

    Is it too much to ask a kid to work hard for just 20 hours? In the 21st century you have two challenges as a coach. One is to find the "throwback" kid who will work hard and not just do the bare minimum required when we all know it takes a greater commitment to be successful. You'll need to find the kid who gives you "$3 of work for $2 pay". The other is to take *all* your kids and find a way for them to reach their full potential.

The NCAA does not allow you to take a kid's scholarship based on athletic performance. That rule is there for good reason. If I recruit a kid, she works hard in the classroom and on the court, and her athletic potential doesn't turn out to be what I thought it would be, I'm okay with that. By all means she should keep her scholarship. But it grinds on my nerves when kids are lazy. Kids should not stand out because they work hard. Shouldn't they all work hard and try to do what's expected because it's the right thing to do?

Coaches will try anything to help an athlete reach his or her full potential. But if all options are exhausted and an athlete isn't internally motivated to be the best, that kid will have much bigger problems to deal with later in life. The unfortunate part for college coaches is that we can't always see that during the recruiting process.

Coaches are extremely loyal people. We will hang in there to the nth degree with our players and our institutions. Unfortunately that loyalty is not always reciprocated. Consider a social climate in the 21st century that is becoming more and more litigious. People sue for the most ridiculous things. Make sure you cover yourself if you are a head coach. One of the best things my financial planner advised me to do is to have an umbrella insurance policy that includes professional liability coverage. It gives you additional protection in case you get sued. This is especially important if you run camps and clinics. Head coaches are high profile people and more likely to be named in a lawsuit if someone sues the athletic department or institution. That little extra you pay each year could save you a lot of heartache financially.

Finally, protect yourself by making sure you and your athletic director are always on the same page with regards to how you handle situations. Have regular meetings and keep them in the loop when you have issues. You don't have to tell them every single thing that goes on with your program. But communicate about major issues because ADs don't like to be blindsided with a phone call from a parent or someone from the media. It makes them look bad.

With the present climate of 21st century athletics you must ask yourself an important question; "How long do I want to coach?" We get older but the kids will always be 18-22. The reality is that things change. And when change occurs coaches have to make a choice--evolve or leave coaching. How much are you willing to change? A friend of mine told

> "To help you decide what's best for you start with your core values and work your way outward. Use them as your compass."

me about a story he read to his six year old son called *A Bad Case of Stripes* by David Shannon. It's about a little girl who doesn't stay true to herself and it causes her problems. It's a simple book that would probably take you five minutes to read but it speaks volumes about making decisions that are right for you personally. To help you decide what's best for you start with your core values and work your way outward. That way you will always keep things in perspective. What is important to you? Is it family? Is it your morals? What makes you you? Your core values are your anchor and they will keep you grounded. Use them as your compass. And if you aren't willing to make the necessary changes, given today's environment, then you need to pursue a different profession. Otherwise you will be doing yourself, your student-athletes, and the people you work with a disservice.

Chapter 15
FOLLOW THE LEADER

One of the toughest aspects of coaching is deciding on your leadership style. Do you lead from the front or from behind? Do you push and prod or let the team develop at its own pace? A coach's personality and his or her team's personality can be totally different. The key is to find a happy medium that fits both, but that's easier said than done. If you coach for the right reasons then your aim should actually be servant leadership. As their coach *you are there to serve the players.* And I don't mean serve as in the "inmates run the asylum". I mean you should have each player's best interest in mind at all times and try to give them what they need to be successful.

> "A coach's personality and his or her team's personality can be totally different. The key is to find a happy medium that fits both."

I had a hard time deciding how I would lead. My natural inclination is to empower my players to think for themselves. I want them to be invested and be independent thinkers. A lot of that philosophy comes from my time as a walk-on at Wake Forest. As someone who didn't log very many minutes I know personally how important it is to make sure everyone feels like they are an important part of the program/process. So my biggest decision was "Do I lead with an inclusive mindset or do I lead with a hierarchal mindset?" In a hierarchy one person is at the top so they are responsible for the vision of the program. Someone has to sit in the big chair and make the final decisions. Leading with an inclusive mindset is about making sure each person (staff and players) feels valued and cared about. Each person needs to be assured they have something to add to the program and that his or her contribution matters. Empowering others strengthens the organization but not everyone is ready for the responsibility and accountability that comes with that. Do your homework before you delegate.

Both types of leaders are important for servant leadership. The problem head coaches run into is that kids need discipline, yet they also need to have the freedom to learn to make good decisions. Kids know they need discipline but don't like when they get it. When I interviewed for my first head coaching job I asked the players what they thought the program needed. They all said discipline and I responded "Be careful what you ask for".

Many times when you take over a program it's necessary to be hierarchal because there needs to be order and structure. You need to have standards and set expectations. Initially kids will push the envelope to test a new coach to see how far they can go and what they can get away with—just like they do with their parents. Remember that you are inheriting kids someone else recruited and it will take time to gain their respect. How you set the tone at the beginning will determine a lot. I took over a program that had three coaches in three years and there were some genuine abandonment issues to deal with. Imagine what those kids were feeling having to get used to three different personalities, systems, and sets of rules. The only solution was to be myself and do what I thought would work best for the program; establish parameters, set boundaries, identify goals, and stress discipline and accountability. As you would imagine, some of the players refused to buy in and we had issues. New coaches can encounter situations like that so it's even more important to be aware of what you are getting yourself into. I was confident in my ability to do the job, but in my naiveté I thought things would work themselves out and it was much more difficult than I had anticipated. That's another reason why you need stable leadership that will be patient and supportive.

I decided it was best to start tough and let go gradually as we progressed. Unless you inherit a mature team with good veteran leadership it will be difficult to accomplish any other way. I don't mean that I was a jerk and abused my players. But I understood that if you lose some kids at the beginning from a lack of discipline you may never get others to follow. In that type of situation you have to make it clear that things will be done your way but try your best to communicate that message in a positive manner. After that you have to be patient. I established a structured environment where I nurtured the ones who bought in and let the ones who resisted know there was a minimum standard of behavior that they would have to adhere to if they expected to stay involved with the team. Needless to say we didn't win very many games at the beginning. The tricky part in situations such as this is to balance being tough with actions that let the kids know you care about them--to know when, where and how much discipline to apply. And boy is that hard. Coaches don't get that right every day. I sure didn't.

Jay Carty, in the book *One On One* he co-authored with John Wooden, describes Coach Wooden's approach to discipline. "Punishment is for the punisher's benefit, to make him or her feel better. Discipline always has the other person's best interest in mind." I believe it's not necessary (nor appropriate) to put your hands on a player in anger or demean them (in public or private). My approach to discipline was to focus on things the players thought I was being picky about; small things like everyone having the same socks on game day or keeping the locker room clean and neat. They griped about the socks but what they didn't understand is that it wasn't even about the socks. It was about making sure you thought about your teammates first; about togetherness. It's exactly what works in the military. Drills are often harsh; rules appear petty and nit-picky. They're really designed to get everyone on board with the program and to work as a unit. It's the same with sports teams. Periodically I would inspect the locker room to make sure the lockers were neat and the door was shut securely because I didn't want the nice things they had to disappear. One day, after repeated reminders, I decided to teach them a lesson. I went into each locker, pulled every piece of clothing out, put them in the middle of the floor and mixed them together (it's something I got from my days at the Naval Academy). Another day I took their cell phones and they were upset because they thought they had been stolen. How on earth would they survive if they could not text?! They were mad. But again, it wasn't about the clothes or the phones. It was about discipline. If they couldn't be disciplined enough to keep their lockers neat and close the door, then how would they be able to make the right decisions on the court (or in life)?

Often head coaches lead a lonely existence but we're just like anybody else; we want to be liked too. Kids never want to ride with the head coach because it's not fun. They always like the assistant coach better because they are generally more positive and may seem more accessible emotionally. Your players need to know you care about them, but sometimes you have to do things in the short term that they don't like because you know it is good for the team (and them) long term. I'm sure you have heard the cliché "kids don't care what you know until they know you care". Well, sometimes being hard on them is how you show that you care. The unfortunate thing for coaches is that many times the tough love that is needed won't be understood or appreciated by the player until years later.

I find that meting out consequences (I never use the word punishment because I want them to understand how reward vs. consequence works in the real world) is the most difficult part of the job for me. There were days I went home feeling awful about the consequences I gave but that's part of the job. I was comfortable with my role as the heavy but I also wanted to be closer to the kids. Fortunately, as the years pass I have grown closer to some of them after they graduated. It is nice that we can have some conversations now that we were not able to have when they were student-athletes.

Sometimes when you take over a program you have to show how willing you are to commit to being a disciplinarian. My first and second year as a head coach I had this kid on my team who was one of the best athletes (male or female) in the entire school. She could out lift a lot of the guys and she really worked hard. She was a great kid who had a beautiful aura about her but she was never held accountable for any of her transgressions by the previous coach, and she tended to act out when she was angry with something or someone. When I arrived I knew that I had to make sure the kids understood how important it was to do the right thing, but I also wanted to let them know I understood people make mistakes. I told them in our first team meeting "If something bad happens I don't have to be the first person you call but I better be the second." That was in May of my first year. In July I received a call on my birthday. It was the end of a great day I had spent shopping at the outlet stores. This kid had gotten in trouble and wanted to let me know.

This situation was my first big test and how I responded would definitely send a signal to others about the way I intended to run the program. At first I was going to suspend her for the semester. When I told my assistant he responded, "Have you lost your mind? That's nine games!" I decided he was right but I still needed to make my point. If I only suspended her for two games, that would be a slap on the wrist for her misconduct. I thought about it and settled on six games and a list of conditions she had to meet in order to get back on the team. She would have to come to practice every day and work hard without complaining and moping. She could not travel to away games but she could sit on the bench at home games and support her teammates. And if she missed even one class the deal was off. I didn't really know the kid well enough to predict whether she would follow through but I was pleasantly surprised. She handled the consequence beautifully and complied with all my conditions.

  The next year that kid continued to have issues with her anger. Finally, during one practice I had had enough and told her that if she didn't correct her behavior I was going to throw her out of the gym. Well of course she had to test me so I threw her out. She left yelling that she was going to quit and never come back. I told the team I wasn't going to chase her and if she wanted to get back on the team she had to come to me. Now I knew the kid was immature and I didn't want her to quit. If she did she wouldn't learn to persevere when she had "real" problems. So I called her mother and told her she needed to come to school and bring her daughter to my office because she was going to risk losing everything and regret it later. The conversation with her and her mother went as follows:

"Who was that person I kicked out of the gym today?"

Between sniffles she replied, "Coach, no one is working hard on this team. I'm the only one."

"Well, what have you done about it?"

"Huh?"

"What have you done about it? I hear you complaining but it doesn't seem like you've done anything to remedy the situation. Did you talk to your teammates?"

"No."

"Do they know how upset you are?"

"No. But they don't care. I'm quitting!"

"So you are going to give up your scholarship because you think the teammates who you haven't spoken with about your concerns don't care? Do you think that's productive?"

No answer.

"Let me tell you what's going on here. You are stubborn. You want what you want, when you want it. And you want to take the easy way out by quitting when things don't go your way."

At this point her mother is sitting in front of me just nodding her head and the kid's eyes pop wide open. This is the first time anyone had actually held her accountable.

"So here's what's going to happen. You are *not* going to quit and I'll tell you why. First of all, we just paid $800 for a plane ticket for you to go to Alaska and you are going on that trip! Second, you are going to tell your teammates how you feel because you probably aren't the only one who feels that way. Third, you are going to apologize to them for your actions. Finally, you are going to come to practice tomorrow and if you want to get back in the gym you will deal with the consequence I give you. And you don't get to ask what that consequence is so you can decide if you want to do it. Is that clear?"

She looked at her mom and her mom said, "Coach, she'll be there."

After that meeting I didn't have any other issues with the kid. My point is that you have to be willing to follow through with discipline (even if it's with your best player), because if you don't it will hurt your standing with the team. I took a risk because the kid could very well have decided she didn't want to come back and that would have really hurt our chances of winning games. But I also knew she was a good kid and I didn't want her to make a decision that would cost her in the future. I also wanted her teammates to understand that I was not going to allow toxic behavior in our program. After graduating that kid became a prison guard. Think she understands my methods now?

One crucial part of leadership coaches often overlook is the leadership from the players. All successful programs have a strong presence in the locker room. Sometimes kids respond more easily to demands from their peers. But the key is to figure out if that presence in the locker room is from influencers or from leaders. Both have followers. The difference is that influencers can have a negative impact. They divide teams and persuade younger players to follow the wrong path. Leaders have a positive effect. They are the ones who organize captains' practices, the ones who think about what the team needs before they go to sleep at night. They speak for and support the coaching staff in the locker room. I usually had two captains on my team because some players have no problem with keeping teammates accountable; some feel better leading by example. Having both types gave the team balance. Every coach would love to have the total package--a kid with street cred (i.e. your best player) who works hard, does things the right way and will call out his or her teammates when needed. But only a few are so fortunate.

I tried to help my players develop leadership skills and be invested in and own their program. Often I would tell them I'm simply a guide; here to provide a template and a vision for what you want to accomplish. This is "your" program. I would use the analogy of the driver's ed teacher. The teacher sits in the passenger seat and gives direction but the student is the one driving the car. The teacher has a brake pedal on their side in case they need to intervene and stop something bad from happening, but it's better if the driver makes good decisions. I wanted my players to take ownership of their program and I constantly used methods like allowing them to plan practice, etc. to help them understand what that means.

Developing team leaders isn't easy. Some kids have the personality to be good leaders and some avoid it like the plague. But I believe all kids have the ability to lead and coaches should help develop and nurture their leadership skills. We can't expect them to do a good job without giving some guidance. There are tons of resources out there to help you help your players. Take advantage of them. And don't be ashamed to bring in someone who can help give them tools to be good leaders. Again it's not about you. It's about the kids and their development.

    There are certain things the head coach must accomplish that demand they take charge and this must be balanced with the desire for everyone to feel like they are part of the process. It's even more difficult with the reality that head coaches are constantly dealing with external stressors on a daily basis that players (and assistants) don't always know about (nor should they). We don't always have a lot of time to explain to everyone that the decisions we make are in the best interest of the program. Sometimes it's "because I said so" and that's it. Many times how you handle alums, donors, and others is a modified version of that, because you can't actually say those words to them (nor should you be thinking that way). You have to be diplomatic yet firm in relaying your view that the way you are handling situations is how you think it is best to do so. Let people know that you are certainly open to hearing what they have to say. You don't want to be perceived as close-minded, egotistical and selfish. But as the head coach you are the only person privy to everything, every aspect of your program. Your decisions are made within that context. Other people base their opinions on the small slice of what they see at a game, a conversation they may have overheard, or something they have read, seen, or heard through the media. You can't let that affect your decision-making. You are ultimately responsible for leading your program; in the end you have to do what you think is right. And if you make mistakes, acknowledge them, learn from them and move on.

If I could lead with an inclusive mindset all the time I would because that's my personality. But that method takes time and it has to be done the right way because kids have to mature and grow into what's expected of them. You have to figure out what fits you as a leader, understanding that you sometimes have to be a chameleon. At times it may involve you stepping out of your comfort zone. The key is to send a clear and consistent message that signals you are a competent leader. And the overriding factor in your decision should be the answer to this question; "What is best for this program at this time?"

Chapter 16

YES MISS…
HOW MAY I HELP YOU TODAY?

When my players called me I would answer the phone with this sentence. And although I was joking it really describes my management style. I always felt the most important part of my job as a coach was to help my players and assistants get better; to teach and help them learn from my successes as well as my mistakes. As coaches we are all educators. We teach people we come in contact with every day. Our classroom just happens to be in the gym or on the field.

As a head coach you will need to decide what your management style is. It will depend on your personality, your background and your life experiences. How you manage the people you work with is important in any profession. But with coaching it's much more difficult because the results can be open ended for a long period of time. Let me explain. In a business there is always a bottom line. A person does his or her job, and if it's done well the company profits. If enough people do a good job the company makes money. The people who do the best work get bonuses, promotions, and raises. There is a measurable end result on which to base those rewards. But in coaching you deal with young people who develop and mature at their own individual pace. You may not be able to definitively measure the end result for up to four years (or more). You see glimpses of progress. Sometimes that progress continues and sometimes a kid takes two steps back for every one forward.

I had a kid on my team who was a tremendous athlete. She was faster with the ball than most people without it and I recruited her because she reminded me a little of myself as a player. She wasn't a great shooter but I didn't care. I knew she could take over a game with her defense and that was what we needed from her. After her freshman year she came to me and said "Coach, I realize now after this year that I should have worked harder in the summer." After that I'm thinking she "gets it" and was going to work really hard over the summer. But the next time I saw her she had gained 15 pounds and was out of shape. She hadn't done anything except eat fast food! I was furious because she couldn't get through preseason workouts, didn't make any times on her sprints and had regressed in the weight room. I had to figure out how I was going to manage the situation, remembering to be aware of my filters. Part of me wanted to pop her upside her head. How could you make that statement to your coach, then three months later report to school out of shape? But I knew that she was too young to share my thought process. So I met with her over the course of the year trying to make sure she knew what was expected of her. Obviously she didn't play much and was frustrated. And of course it was my fault that she wasn't playing. "I know, but…" In our end of the year meeting I finally told her she should find another place to play. Well this created an uproar. Like most immature kids she played the victim and everyone thought I was the monster. But I had not come to this decision lightly and I knew people would be mad at me. Honestly I didn't really want her to leave. I never really intended to take her scholarship. But I had tried everything I could think of to get her to understand why it was important to fulfill her responsibilities and felt there was no other way to get her attention. She didn't understand that her lack of performance was affecting my bottom line. I agonized and lost sleep over my decision. But it would have been unfair to the other kids on the team who did put in their time for me not to address the situation.

    The kid and I didn't speak much for the first couple of weeks after school ended that year. During that time I thought about the situation nonstop. I realized that I was still mad at her and that was not productive. I knew that I would have to extend the olive branch so I told her we were going to meet once a week. That first meeting I told her that the reason I wanted to get together was twofold; one, I needed to get to know her better so that I could see why she decided to spend the previous summer eating fast food and not working out; two, my anger was blocking my own and the team's blessings and that had to stop. When I met with her I was careful not to do it in a way where she felt intimidated. I wanted her to be comfortable enough to share her thoughts. Sometimes we met in the student union building. Or if we met in my office I made sure not to sit behind my desk. I didn't want any figurative or literal barriers between us when I shared personal aspects of my life hoping she would open up.

That whole exercise was particularly difficult for me because I grew up believing that you always earned what you got. No one ever talked to me about why I wasn't performing. But it helped her open up to me and I was able to understand her a little more. The next season she came back in better shape. She was inconsistent but I could see she was trying to improve. In fact, she was the reason we won a couple of really huge games that year. She still didn't completely have the work ethic we needed but I saw progress. In her senior season she really came on strong. She worked out all summer and returned fit, ready to go. I think it was a combination of that natural sense of urgency seniors have and her maturity level. She became a starter and her performance on defense set the tone for our team all season. It was amazing to see her finally realize how important she was to the team and how much she could impact a game with her skills. I cannot articulate how proud I was of her by the time she graduated. I tell that story to illustrate that managing people is a crucial component of leadership but not everyone will process leadership the same way. There are some kids who function well when you're constantly on them to get their s_ _ t in gear. They want you to yell at them. Others need a softer approach-no yelling, just constant positive reinforcement. I will admit that, given my background, the latter is something I had to get used to doing.

There are times you may have to adjust your management style for each kid. Everyone should get treated fairly but not necessarily the same. For instance, I handled policy infractions on a case-by-case basis. Let's use class attendance again as an example. Sometimes I checked class in person; sometimes I would email the professors. But many times I would see the professors in a social setting and they would always volunteer how my kids were performing because they knew how important it was to me.

One night I was watching our men's basketball team play with a group of friends, one of whom happened to be my player's math professor. We were chatting and he casually mentioned that she had missed class that week. He wasn't trying to get her in trouble. It just came up in the course of conversation. The kid was at the game as well so I walked across the gym after it was over and had a conversation that went something like this:

"Is there something you need to tell me?"

"No, Coach."

"You sure?"

"Yeah, I'm sure."

"You positive?"

"Yeah, I'm positive."

"Well, look who I sat next to at the game tonight."

Her face turned beet red and she immediately began to explain in stream of consciousness sentences.

"Aw man! Coach, I had class all morning and we were leaving for our game early in the afternoon and I was hungry and knew that you wouldn't want me not to eat a pre-game meal on game day because you always say we need to think of our teammates and take care of our bodies and I wanted to make sure I had enough energy for the game since I play a lot and there was no time to eat and go to class and I didn't really miss anything and I have an A in the class anyway."

I responded "Hmmm. So what you are telling me is that you didn't do a good job of having foresight and planning your day, right?"

"Coach, what is my consequence going to be?"

I don't remember exactly what consequence I gave her but I'm sure it was enough for the other players on my team to get the message about priorities.

Another kid missed class and I handled her differently. I had been on her case for almost a year about making academics a priority because she was always flirting with eligibility issues. I found out she was flying home to an event one weekend and told her that she needed to make sure she didn't miss any class before or after her trip. She promised that she wouldn't. The weekend passed, I decided to check with her professors and found out she missed more than one class. I called her in the office and our conversation went as follows:

"Where were you Friday morning for your 8:00 A.M. class?"

"Uh, I don't know." (I promise that really was her answer!)

"You don't know? How can you not know where you were?"

"Coach, I don't remember."

"Hmmm. Okay. Where were you Monday morning for your 9:00, 10:00, and 11:00 A.M. classes?"

"Uh, eating breakfast."

"You were eating breakfast for that long?"

Silence. "So we agreed you wouldn't miss class and you deliberately violated team policy. I thought we discussed how important your academics are."

More silence.

She finally tried to tell me that she couldn't get a flight back in time. I didn't allow her to make that excuse because I knew she had gotten the ticket well in advance of her trip and she knew exactly what she was doing. I suspended her from practice for two days and from the next game. I told her she would spend that time in supervised study hours equal to the amount of time she missed class (in addition to the normal study hall hours I required for the team). The difference between the two kids was that the first kid was so smart she could have skipped all her classes the entire semester and probably still would have made an A. The second one didn't have any margin for error based on her previous performance in the classroom. Still, I had to discipline both.

Sometimes you have to be creative when you manage discipline so that it registers more clearly with your players. For example, one of my players violated a very important team rule. She was out late and I had always told my kids nothing good happens when you're out past 12:00 A.M. Of course something bad happened and her parents had to drive a long distance to come take care of her. Thankfully the parents were on my side and told me I had every right to discipline her any way I saw fit. I decided that the normal consequence would not be sufficient. So I waited until the next weekend and told her that after her last class on Friday she had to check in with me every hour by phone until the time she had gotten in trouble the previous weekend. I told her I might answer the phone, I might not; but she had better make sure and call me. Basically she had to call me every hour from 3:00 P.M. that Friday until 3:00 A.M. Sunday morning. And if she missed even one phone call she would have to do it all over again the next weekend. You can imagine the fatigue and worry in her voice as she called me in the wee hours wondering if I had gotten the message. But I wanted her to be stressed and worried the entire time so she would know what her parents and I felt like. My methods got her attention--as well as the attention of the other kids on the team.

In each scenario I gave the individual a consequence so it would be clear to my players that I was serious about them keeping the team a priority and following the rules. While each kid was treated differently, I believe they all were treated fairly. These examples show how difficult it is to "schedule" end results (whether it's academics, maturity, etc) in athletics. These results come when they come and we have to deal with it.

Managing expectations of your players is also hard. I always thought leading by example and exhibiting the behavior I expected of my players would be enough. But that was not the case so I had to find different ways of communicating my expectations. I delegated a lot of responsibility to my players because I didn't have a large staff. There were a couple of things I did to make sure my players stayed accountable. Everyone was assigned a "buddy". Each set of kids was responsible for making sure their partner was reliable so that the coaches didn't have to continually preach the concept of accountability. Sometimes if one buddy screwed up I would ask "Who is your buddy?"

and the other buddy would have to pay the price. You would be amazed at how quickly that instilled discipline. After my first couple of years I gave my captains a lot of responsibility. They knew our policies and were in charge of making sure everyone followed them. Those kids knew me well enough, what I would allow and what drove me nuts. By my fifth year the captains were in charge of going over the policy manual with new players. I also let them be a part of the decision making process in areas I felt they could handle. Captains were always responsible for deciding what type of gear we would wear. They got to decide where and what time we ate and sometimes what time and how long we would practice. I wanted them to feel like I trusted them so I was consistent when I delegated responsibilities. If the captains came to me during the second half of the season and said the team was tired I listened. But I also let them know that they had to be accountable with my trust. They were responsible for making sure the team worked hard if I decided to trim practice time.

Head coaches have to manage staff as well as players and it's not any easier. There are so many factors to consider regarding how you deal with each person you hire. One of the most important is that you be aware of those critical skills I mentioned earlier. You have to be honest and know yourself in order to figure out what kind of staff you need.

For my first hire as a head coach I knew I was only going to get one assistant. I had to evaluate my own strengths in order to figure out what I needed in an assistant. I felt I would be fine with promoting the program and building the relationships we would need to be successful. What I needed was someone who was great at and took pride in accomplishing things behind the scenes. I needed someone who was a grinder and who I didn't have to constantly monitor. Later on, when I hired an assistant for the second time, both the program and I had evolved so there was a different need. I was getting older so I needed to hire someone younger to bridge the generation and communication gaps. Her job was to let me know if the things I didn't understand needed to be addressed by me or if I was just being "old".

I felt like my job was to help groom my assistants so I kept that in mind when I interacted with them. My management style with assistants was to hire good people and let them do their job. I didn't want to have to micromanage them because I was too busy dealing with all the stuff head coaches deal with; the budget, scheduling, donors, or an AD who may be a micromanager themselves. My feeling was that if I had to look over your shoulder every five minutes then I shouldn't have hired you in the first place.

I am a big picture kind of person. A typical conversation with my assistant would involve me telling them what end result I wanted, the parameters I wanted them to use and a time frame in which to get it done. "I don't know how you are going to get from A to Z, but this is what I want, why I want it and when I need it." Then I would leave them alone. My natural inclination was to want projects finished earlier than I asked for because I always beat my deadlines when I was an assistant. But I stuck to the time frame I gave and allowed them to figure out how best to accomplish the task on their own. Of course, to do that you would have to hire a mature coach if you only have one position. If you have more than one slot you have the luxury of working with and helping people develop at various stages in their careers.

I liked to keep it pretty simple. I made it clear that my assistant's job was to always have an answer when I had a question. If they didn't, then they had better find the answer. My assistants were free to express their opinions with the understanding that I would listen, but once I made the final decision they had to be on board outside the office. There will always be times when an assistant feels strongly about an issue and will make repeated attempts to sway your opinion. When that happened I usually gave one of two answers; "Coach, I got it. Thank you!" or "When you get to sit in the big chair you can do what you want. But I'm the head coach and my decision is final." I didn't mind when my assistants spoke up because sometimes they had better ideas. They just needed to do it in the appropriate manner.

To help my assistants grow I made sure that they ran drills so that the kids knew they were capable coaches. I didn't miss many practices but every once in a while I would have to go see a recruit or be in a meeting and I didn't want the kids to feel like they were going to have it easy when I was not around. I wanted them to respect my assistants and the only way to accomplish that was to let them coach. They also needed that experience so they could prepare for the day when they would sit in the big chair. The hardest part for me was during timeouts in games. I liked to evaluate the situation, make a decision and then tell the kids what we were going to do. That seems oxymoronic given that I prefer to delegate and empower the people I work with. But early in my career I thought since I was the one who would be judged on wins and losses (and it was my butt that was on the line), I should be the one to make the final decision on what we did. It took me a while

> "...as a head coach you never cede your authority."

to realize the advantage of talking things over with my assistants, understanding they sometimes see things I don't.

In my mind, the better the assistants became the more successful the program would be. Sometimes that worked and sometimes it didn't. I learned that no matter how much responsibility you give an assistant, the kids ultimately want to hear your "voice" and they want the head coach to take charge. And I also learned that as a head coach you never cede your authority. You don't want a situation where the kids aren't sure who to listen to. That creates all sorts of problems in the program. It's a delicate balance empowering the people who work for you while retaining your authority and respect from the players and your staff.

My interviews with candidates were very long and detailed because I needed to make sure that the person I hired could flourish and help us be successful in the environment I typically fostered. The interview process for my searches usually lasted an entire work day and I structured it that way on purpose. Usually the candidate would arrive in the morning and his or her schedule would go something like this:

-Meet with people in administration

-Tour of campus with a couple of players

-If we were in a period where we could work out players I would have the candidate coach them through a workout

-Question and answer session with team captains

-Chalk talk with me

-A mock recruiting call with me posing as the recruit

-Have them write a recruiting letter

-Question and answer session with me on topics other than basketball. I would ask behavior-based questions; presenting them with scenarios and asking how they would handle the situation. Or I would ask them their views on NCAA or athletic issues. Their answers would give me insight into their thought processes and help me gauge what type of person they were.

-Have them write a separate practice schedule for preseason, in season, and postseason

-Scouting report (Sometime during the interview I would give the candidate DVDs of an opponent and tell them to write a scouting report in two hours. I didn't let them know this beforehand.)

Whew! That's a lot. But I wanted to see what they could handle. Could they perform under pressure? Did they have a good basketball IQ? How did they handle things they weren't aware they were going to have to do? Were they personable? Did the kids feel comfortable with them? Were they articulate? Could they write well? All of these things were important for me to discern because of my management style.

The key for me was to hire people who had strengths in the areas I didn't. That's smart hiring. Don't be afraid to hire someone who is good at coaching in an area you may not know very well and who you can learn from. And if you are an older coach don't be afraid to hire younger coaches who can help bridge the communication gap. I'm from the generation that had 8 track tapes, 45 and 33 records, and TVs with rabbit ears and knobs for changing channels. Some of the stuff my kids did I just didn't understand so it made sense for me to hire someone who could. Conversely, if you're a young coach don't have such a big ego that you dismiss the value of hiring an "old head" on your staff. Their experience can help guide you and keep you out of trouble. Finally, hire someone who shares your values but not necessarily your opinion. You don't want "yes" people. You want people who will be invested in your program's success and won't be afraid to tell you what they think.

One final and crucial aspect of managing is dealing with the people you report to. This is often referred to as "managing up". Many times coaches don't understand or realize that you have to cultivate your relationships with the administration just as you would a recruit, a parent, or another coach. Have regular communication with those to whom you report. This was especially important to me when I experienced a lot of turnover in my leadership. One day I was complaining to a mentor of mine about my AD not understanding me. He told me to go to lunch with that person. "Why do I need to go to lunch?" I asked. He responded, "Because you need to have conversation on a regular basis so you can get to know each other. You don't always want to go to your AD when you want something or when there is a problem. It's an informal way to help you both develop trust." Sharing a meal is a simple thing but it makes a whole lot of sense because it allows two people to communicate in an environment where both feel comfortable. One time I was having lunch with my interim AD and he presented me with an email that had been sent to him by an angry alumna. She was not happy with the performance of the team and questioned my hiring, noting that many alumnae were dissatisfied. He asked what I thought and I think my answer surprised him. My response was "I'm happy that they care enough to express how they feel about their program. I'm not satisfied either and we are all working hard to get this program back to where it belongs." Had I been in his office or he in mine, I might have responded differently.

When we lead programs our job is to take care of our players and staff. We are laser focused on their needs. But we should also realize that an AD has *every* team to think about and their decisions are made with the entire department in mind. Understand that ADs go through processes to make decisions on requests and the "no" they sometimes give you is not personal.

There is no single way of managing that works for everyone because we all have different personalities and different circumstances. If you are not sure of your approach do some research by reading about different styles and talking to people in your network. Figure out what management style works best for you and cultivate it.

Chapter 17
COACH, WHAT DOES THIS HAVE TO DO WITH BASKETBALL?

Coaches spend so much time working to win games we often lose sight of one of our main jobs; the obligation to get our players ready to navigate and be successful in the real world. It's important that kids master three attributes: discipline, responsibility, and accountability. And as I have mentioned before it's crucial for the coaching staff to set the tone by modeling those behaviors. Nothing less than 100% in each area should be accepted from your players or your staff. That's something that will take time for the players to understand. It's important that you be consistent (and fair) in your demands. If you tolerate disrespect, tardiness, laziness, etc then you can expect to be part of a losing program. Demand that each kid strive to reach their personal best in every way and they will eventually meet your expectations. And let them know that expectations are mutual. If they expect us to be accountable as coaches and teachers, be sure we expect them to be accountable as student-athletes.

Sometimes we do too much for our kids because we want to help. They need to know we are always available, but we should at least encourage them to attempt to be part of the solutions to their problems. Self-reliance is a key component to survival and success. Sometimes when we tell a kid stuff a gazillion times it seems like such a waste of time. But think back to when you were in college. Were you really all that different? We didn't listen as much as we should have either. Don't be surprised if a kid who has graduated comes back to you because they still need your help. They go out into the real world and experience what you tried to tell them was going to happen and they realize you were right. All of a sudden you are smart. When that happens, don't gloat. Just be there for them. Mark Twain wrote: "When I was fourteen, my father was the dumbest person I ever met. By the time I turned twenty-one, I was amazed at how much the old man had learned in seven years. Oh, the folly of youth!"

It's incredible what one can achieve simply by believing in one's ability to do so. We have to do a good job of communicating this to our kids. Helping build self-esteem is especially important in coaching whether you are

> "Helping build self-esteem is especially important in coaching whether you are coaching men or women."

coaching men or women. It can help determine a kid's place in a world that has become increasingly competitive in every aspect of life. You hope kids have some measure of self-confidence when they arrive on your team, but there's no way to tell for sure. Kids are great actors. They can project an exterior of strength and confidence while they are struggling internally with both. And that can manifest itself on the court, on the field, or in the classroom. Numbers don't lie. Kids can talk all they want about what they will do. Results are results. But the kids won't always come to you because sometimes they don't know how to ask for help. You have to figure out a way to help them feel comfortable discussing their issues. Don't be egotistical. If there is someone else who is qualified that they feel more comfortable opening up to, let them know it is okay to communicate with that person. The last thing you want is for their issues not to be resolved because you felt like you were the only person in the world who could help them. Get over yourself and understand it's the kid's well-being that is most important.

Developing self-esteem and confidence can be the difference between a complete player who reaches his or her full potential (academically/athletically) and one who remains mediocre for his or her entire career (or life). But it's difficult to be patient with kids' development in this area because our jobs as coaches are dependent upon their performance. We preach that instant gratification is not how real life works, yet we are under constant pressure to produce exactly that for our bosses and fans. I had several changes in athletic and institutional leadership during my tenure as head coach. It wasn't until after I lost my job that I realized how much an effect the stress of dealing with the turnover had on my communication with my kids and with their overall performance. Coaching is a demanding profession and we have to balance dealing with those demands and being patient with the growth of our players as people. It's not an easy task.

    I used a variety of tactics to help my players grow on and off the court. One of the first things I did was to raise money to take them on trips outside our region. I have always believed that traveling enhances a student's education. Young people must embrace cultural differences rather than shy away from (or worse, be indifferent to) them. By traveling, kids are exposed to different lifestyles. This enables them to form their own opinions and leads to a richer, fuller sense of awareness. Interaction with different cultures allows them to grow vertically (obtaining their degrees) and horizontally (broadening their perspectives in life).

Traveling to different places with my players was both important and personal to me. As a student-athlete and a coach, exposure to new things has significantly broadened my world view. I took my first trip overseas when I worked at Princeton. We took the team to Scandinavia and spent ten days in Sweden, Denmark, and Norway. It was a phenomenal experience for me for many reasons. During our layover in the airport in Paris I had to remember the French I was taught in my fourth grade Catholic school class to communicate with people and figure out the exchange rate for the Euro. Our itinerary included more than playing basketball. We played six games in that time span, but our preparation consisted of showing up for the game, talking about what we wanted to do, warming up and playing. Every kid got an opportunity to play and we worked on the things we wanted to accomplish during the upcoming season. When we were not playing we toured, shopped, and took in the local environment. Again I had to learn to use a different currency because each country has its own monetary system.

Experiencing a different culture helped me realize how much we take for granted in our country. When I went to the grocery stores I noticed that there were only a few choices for most items. In the U.S. we have so many different brands for each item of merchandise. Do we really need all of them? And it seemed to me everything was more compact overseas. The cars and rooms were small; every inch of space was accounted for. Those were just some of the interesting things I noticed that helped me to see the world differently. I wanted my players to have their own unique experiences.

We traveled to several places with our kids and in each place we exposed them to new and different cultural opportunities. In Alaska I noticed all the cars had plugs protruding from the hoods. I asked my player from Alaska why and she explained that it gets so cold in Alaska that they have to plug their cars in so the batteries don't freeze. So you see poles with outlets on them and garages with outlets installed for that very reason. What an interesting fact! We visited the Alaska Pipeline and they rode dog sleds. We visited the Space Needle in Seattle and spent time with a former player I coached who works for the FBI. I asked her to bring her son to the visit because I wanted them to see that it is possible to pursue your career and still have a family. We visited the Louisville Slugger Bat Factory, the Muhammad Ali Museum and toured Churchill Downs in Kentucky because I thought it was important to share some historical context with them. Now when my players hear about those things on the news or see them on the internet or in books, they can actually say they have experienced them firsthand.

My other reason for traveling is that I had visions of competing in the NCAA tournament and I knew that if we were to accomplish that we might not be playing close to home. I wanted my kids to understand and be used to what it meant to fly across the country on an airplane, stay in a hotel, be on a schedule for meals and practice and play in an unfamiliar environment.

During the season I would give my kids pop quizzes. I never gave them a playbook because I had seen too many kids leave them behind on road trips. Plus, you don't always have time to write things down when you make adjustments during the course of a game. When I walked into pre-practice with index cards I would give them a certain amount of time and require them to draw up plays or give me a list of things I felt was important for them to be thinking about. This served two purposes. One, it let me know who could perform under pressure. Two, if they drew up plays and they all made mistakes in the same area, then that was my fault as a teacher. I wasn't communicating things well and needed to make corrections.

Another thing I did was to have my kids read books over the summer and write papers. They did not always appreciate that because they thought it had nothing to do with basketball. But it had everything to do with them learning to communicate. I used to take their papers and correct them with a red pen, just like their professors. And there were a lot of corrections because some of them wrote exactly like they texted. For me it was a way to see if they could intelligently transfer their thoughts to paper. If they could, there was a reasonable assumption that they could communicate verbally. Sometimes I would give each kid the name of someone in the news they knew nothing about and make them research that person and write a report. I did this because they rarely paid attention to anything outside their world and I didn't want them to be oblivious to important occurrences that could directly affect their future.

   It's a difficult task helping kids become adults. Sometimes coaches are asked to do in four years what parents haven't done in 18 years and it can be very frustrating. But from the moment you commit to coaching a kid you have a responsibility to help him or her become a productive citizen on and off the court or field, on and off campus, before and after graduation.

Chapter 18

WOOSAH!

After you get a job (especially a head coaching job) the one thing you need to remember to do is to breathe. The morning I accepted my head coaching job I was excited and happy. But I remember later that day sitting in my car and having an anxiety attack. I began to panic thinking, "What if I suck and don't win any games?" That lasted for about five minutes. After I counted to 10 several times and began breathing again I asked myself, "What's the worst thing that could happen? Well, if I don't win enough games I get fired. If that's the worst thing that happens to me in my life then I'll be okay". Little did I know I was foreshadowing my future! But that calmed my nerves and I was able to get to work. I learned several things after becoming a head coach that you just can't know until you sit in the big chair, but I use these lessons in my daily life as well.

Have Patience. Not everything is going to happen when you think it should. Everyone has a schedule in their head of how their career should progress. Guess what? You're not always in control! Remember that quotation by Robin

Roberts about God's delays? We don't always get what we want when we want it. Sometimes what we want isn't supposed to happen. Often our destiny is greater than we could ever imagine. We just need to get out of our own way to achieve it.

Winning Is Important But... Winning or losing games should not define who you are as a person. And even though that should apply to everyone I would venture to say that coaches who don't win many games say that much more than those who do. No matter how you rationalize it, it is awful when you lose. You feel horrible when you put your heart and soul into something and it doesn't turn out the way you imagined it would. But you know what? Life isn't fair. I read a great quotation from the speaker Tony Robbins, "Expecting the world to treat you fair because you are a good person is like expecting a bull not to charge you because you are a vegetarian." So win or lose, live your life.

Have a Strong Sense of Self. Everyone will think they can coach your team better than you. You need thick skin in the coaching profession (and in life). Go to work every day and try to do the right thing. But *never, ever* base your opinion of yourself on someone else's perception of you.

Keep Knocking. So many times people give in to doubt when they encounter obstacles; some literal, some figurative, many created by themselves. Whenever I feel passionate about something I pursue it even though I may have doubts. To me pursuing my passion is no different than securing any other necessity in life. I consider it the food that nourishes my soul. And I believe that if something is on my mind and in my heart every day, then there is a reason for that. So when one door closes I keep "knocking" until the one I need opens.

> "...when one door closes I keep 'knocking' until the one I need opens."

Try Not to Make the Same Mistake Twice. Nobody is perfect. We all make mistakes. And even though it doesn't feel good mistakes help us grow. Learning from those mistakes is important. I always think of the saying "Insanity is doing the same thing over and over again and expecting a different result." Don't be stubborn and think you are always right. It's okay to admit when you are wrong. It's okay to be human.

Try Not to Make a Mistake So Big it Ruins Your Career. We all have that inner voice telling us when things aren't right. Be smart. Listen to it. It only takes one small indiscretion to ruin a career.

Forgive Yourself. You are not always going to do or say the right things so lighten up on yourself. Many a night I lay awake worried because of something I said to a kid or the way I handled a situation only to go to work the next day and the kid had either forgotten, moved on, or forgiven me. Don't beat yourself up. It's wasted energy you could be using elsewhere in a more productive way.

Appreciate The Good Times. Coaches forget to "live life" sometimes. A perfect example of this is how I handled my team beating the #1 team in the country. I let myself enjoy the win only for the amount of time it took to ride the bus home that night and then my thoughts immediately went to what I needed to do for the next game. My players had just experienced arguably one of the biggest moments in their lives and, although I was extremely happy for and proud of them, I didn't allow myself to fully experience their joy. I think about that and hope that in the future I won't forget to be "present" in the moment.

Relax. If you're doing all that you can your dedication will make you successful eventually, whether it's with what you are doing now or something else. Don't be discouraged by failure. It's better to try and fail than to sit and wonder what could have been "if only..." Failure is a necessary part of life. After I retired from coaching it took me five years before I finally had clarity on what I wanted to accomplish. And I never would have gotten there without the failures I experienced along the way.

Enjoy. Being a coach is a privilege, an honor and a blessing. How many people are lucky enough to get paid to do something they enjoy? Be grateful you get to do what you love even though the path is not always smooth. And be sure to remember that on your worst day, when nothing goes right, there is always someone worse off.

Chapter 19
PINK SLIP

"We're going to make a change." "We've decided to go in a different direction." If you haven't heard these words as a coach you're very fortunate. But just because you haven't heard them up to now doesn't mean you won't. Coaching in the 21st century is a business (especially in college). And unfortunately getting let go is part of the profession. Whether it's justified doesn't change anything. No one likes to be let go, especially when they are passionate about their work and loyal to their institution and kids. I always told my kids that if a job doesn't get done there will be consequences and that no one cares about any issues you have. Valid or not, those issues can be used to let you go. Whether it's a new AD who didn't hire you, some kids or parents who don't like you and the job you are doing, or you just don't win enough, it's all the same. I lost my job

> "I realized I wasn't the first coach to ever lose a job, I would not be the last coach to ever lose a job and if I decided to stay in the profession it might not be the last time that happened to me."

twice; once as an assistant and once as a head coach. I realized I wasn't the first coach to ever lose a job, I would not be the last coach to ever lose a job and if I decided to stay in the profession it might not be the last time that happened to me. That's why it's so important to be educated, well rounded and to take care of you. Sometimes coaches know when they are going to be let go and sometimes it's a complete surprise. Whatever the case there are some really important things we should do to make sure we are prepared. That sounds harsh, but it's inherent in a profession where a leader's success is dependent upon the performance of 18-22 year olds. I think sometimes we lose sight of that because we are so passionate for the profession.

Have An Exit Strategy. This seems like a pessimistic outlook but I just think it's prudent in the 21st century. In the old days people worked for one company for 30 years, then retired and lived on a guaranteed pension. Now the days of working for only one company in your lifetime are long gone and you're lucky if you have a pension at all. People have two, sometimes three career changes before they retire. Sometimes those changes don't come voluntarily. They get fired or laid off. It's no different in coaching. We may coach for over 20 years but it's not going to be at the same institution anymore. There are too many expectations for quick fixes and winning records. To remind myself of this every year I read a book called *Who Moved My Cheese* by Spencer Johnson. Usually I read it in August when I am taking some time off to prepare myself for the upcoming school year. It reminds me that the only constant in life is change and it helps me to keep my third eye open. When I started coaching, I knew I didn't want to be 65 and still coaching just because I didn't know what else to do with my life. I wanted coaching to be something I enjoyed, not to be all of who I was. So when I lost my head coaching job I wasn't too anxious initially because I had just begun planning my exit strategy (financially and with my future career aspirations). I was where I had planned to be five years in the future, albeit involuntarily. All I had to do was act on the plan I had begun to put in place. The only bad part was that I wasn't quite where I wanted to be financially and in retrospect had not started the planning process early enough in my career. The scary part was that I turned down two coaching offers (one where I could have made more money than I did as a head coach) without having a job. In a way I felt like I was being tested; like the universe was saying, "You say you don't want to coach anymore? Well let's see if you're really serious about it with these safe, lucrative offers! Are you truly willing to follow your plan?" I said no to the offers because I didn't want to coach anymore. I knew I couldn't commit fully (mentally or physically) to what it would take to help a program be successful and it would not be fair to take a job just for the money. That didn't make it any less frightening.

Trust me, at some point in your life you *will* have to reinvent yourself. When I lost my job I realized that I had not interviewed for a job outside of coaching for over 20 years. I had to update my skill set for the real world so I took computer classes, revised my resume and cover letter, learned and cultivated new social networking skills. You will always need an exit strategy, but not necessarily because you expect to be fired. It is just good to be proactive with your career. So like Stephen Covey says in his book *The Seven Habits of Highly Effective People*, "Begin with the end in mind".

Prepare Yourself Financially. Coaching can be an unstable profession so I enlisted the help of a financial planner early in my career. She and I mapped out my goals and targeted specific ways to achieve them. One thing that is recommended for people in any profession is to have 3-6 months' salary saved. Some call it an emergency fund; others call it a rainy day fund. I call mine the "Go To Hell" fund; aptly named because I have a habit of expressing my opinion when I feel the need to do so (in diplomatic fashion, of course!). I wanted to be prepared in case there would come a day when my boss would tell me to "go to hell" (figuratively speaking, of course!). On my monthly financial statements there is actually a category labeled "GTH". I really think coaches should put one year's salary away. That's not easy, but no matter how small the amount, save money for the future. Because when you lose a job you will have all kinds of new expenses--gas for your car, car payment/insurance, and health insurance (COBRA is expensive!). After I lost my job I initially lived off my GTH fund. I would not have made it financially if I had not put that money away.

Have Your Own Cell Phone, Vehicle and Property. The perks of coaching in college can be really nice. You get a Smartphone to use, a car to drive, maybe a laptop or IPad, and in some cases a place to live. But as quickly as those things are given they can be taken away. When I was let go my phone and car were retrieved immediately. Fortunately I had taken my own advice. I had purchased a condo, come into the 21st century and bought an IPhone, and always kept my personal car in great shape. Don't get lazy and lulled into a false sense of security. When schools let you go they sever ties quickly--no more email, insurance benefits, etc. You cease to exist. It's like you never worked there.

Have Representation. There should always be an open line of communication between you and your athletic director where you can have frank and honest conversation. But when you accept a job there are contractual details that need to be worked out. How that is done may depend on the level at which you coach. At Division I it's pretty standard to use a lawyer in the negotiations. At the other levels it depends on the philosophy of and your relationship with your AD. When you get that opportunity to be a head coach your head is in the clouds because you've finally obtained something you've worked really hard for and you just want to get to work. But you should retain counsel as a resource because that keeps emotions from interfering with civil discourse. Normally I dealt directly with my AD but on the day I was told I would be let go I calmly got up and left his office because I knew that some conversations needed to be had and I should not be the one talking.

Rein In Your Emotions. It's natural to have roller coaster emotions when you are let go. Your feelings go from anger to depression to doubt to anxiety to hope and back again. It's okay to have those feelings but you can't be overwhelmed by any of them. Anger is a normal emotion initially, but it becomes wasted energy after a while that should eventually be used in a more productive way. And depression doesn't always manifest itself in a clinical sense where you need help (although that may be the case). When I mention that, I'm merely speaking of the self-examination you inevitably will go through as you wonder where you failed and what you could have done better to have been successful. You are disappointed things didn't work out the way you envisioned. It's natural to doubt. It's fine to be uncertain. It's also okay not to have all the answers. Because we are so used to solving the problems of our players and staff, this growth process (which is simply part of the life journey that we are all on) is difficult. When my mind would start to drift too far with negative thoughts I would read one of my favorite books *Oh! The Places You'll Go* by Dr. Seuss. Such simple writing can sometimes bring clarity to your thought process. Anxiety is the hardest emotion to deal with because of the unknown. And for me most of that came from financial concerns. I lost my job in the midst of a bad economy but I was never overly anxious about being able to eventually find a job (Okay, I did get a little worried). But head coaches have a lot of responsibilities. We sell, recruit, balance budgets, coordinate travel, raise money, counsel kids, hire and supervise large groups of people, and have a ton of other duties. Coaches have many transferrable skills that can help them be successful in sales, teaching, motivational speaking, consulting, administration, managing corporations, and a whole host of other professions. I was confident that my skill set (and my educational background) would be valuable to someone somewhere.

Continue to Take Care of Yourself. The last thing you want to do is let yourself go. Some coaches don't eat, sleep, or exercise when they lose their job. You must continue to attend to your spirituality, your body and your mind. I'm a firm believer that stress and anxiety can block your blessings. Being unemployed is very stressful and you need to manage that stress so it doesn't negatively affect your psyche. I had to (needed to) reclaim my body, my mind and my spirit. So I increased my workouts because I had more time. I ate healthy meals (for the most part) at home since I was on a budget. And I joined the YMCA so that I could keep myself accountable and be around positive people. Since I no longer had coaching as a competitive outlet I decided to learn how to swim. I plan to train and compete in biathlons in the future. But I also used the challenge of overcoming my fear of water so that it would give me confidence that I could overcome the fear of the unknown. In a sense I replaced one fear with another but it was extremely helpful to focus on something I could control rather than what I couldn't. To keep my mind sharp I made every Monday through Friday like a regular workday. I would exercise in the morning, then go to the library or other places that had free WI-FI, bring my laptop and spend the hours looking for jobs, making phone calls to network, etc. I also finally took the time to write this book. The worst thing you can do is to stay home all day. I went to work every day but for the first time in my life I was working for myself.

See the Time Off as a Blessing and an Opportunity. When I lost my job I had been coaching college basketball for over 20 years. I viewed it as something positive. First of all, it was the first time in a long time that I was the only person on the agenda for the day when I woke up. I had spent so much time taking care of others it was kind of weird at first. But then I began to enjoy the time I had to spend on myself. I was the only appointment on the calendar and there were so many things that I would always plan to work on in the off-season but never actually got to complete. I took classes, started a business and began learning another language. I reinvented myself and worked so that from then on I would be in charge of changing directions with my career path. Use the time off wisely and work on you for a change. The key is to be productive every day. And although it was not my choice, the time off allowed me to rest. We coaches go, go, go all the time and don't realize how tired we are until we are forced to rest (either because we are sick or from something else). If it were possible I would highly recommend that every college coach take a year off to reassess, recalibrate, and rejuvenate. Many coaches who have been in the business for a long time may want to make a change but are afraid. We get used to the lifestyle, the money and freedom of the profession. We don't want to be "boxed in" with the constraints of a "real job" where we do the same thing and see the same people every day. And there are risks involved in changing directions that not everyone is comfortable with. But I'll share what my mother told me when I lost my job. I had been talking for a while about making a change but kept procrastinating by saying I didn't have enough money saved in my GTH account. She told me that if I wanted to do something different I would have to create a vacuum for that opportunity; that I would have to quit coaching. And she said that if it was genuinely in my heart to make that change a vacuum would be created anyway-whether I did it or it happened some other way. I thought that was pretty sage advice.

Continue Professional Development. Sometimes your first thought when you lose your job is that you don't want to coach anymore. If that's truly the case, make sure it's because that's really what you want and not a knee jerk reaction to your situation. Don't be embarrassed to go to your convention. You still need professional development regardless of what profession you choose. And when you do decide on the next step in your career it's likely you will need some extra training anyway. If you still don't want to coach after being around all that basketball/football/volleyball, etc. then that's cool. Don't be afraid to put yourself out there, meet new people, and expose yourself to new experiences. You may find you have a gift for something you never would have pursued otherwise.

Don't Isolate Yourself from People Who Care. Families are the only people whose love for you is unconditional and not dependent upon wins, losses or playing time. Go home and soak up their love. Seek advice from people you know who have been through a similar situation. Also, try volunteering so you won't focus solely on yourself all the time. I volunteered with the media for a first round game of the NCAA tournament and helped run a road race for a company in my area. Find something that interests you and take the focus off yourself.

Leave with Your Dignity and Integrity Intact. The last thing you want to do is give the person who let you go a reason to say, "See, I told you so". You don't need your anger to be misplaced. It took me many months before my anger subsided. To this day I still struggle with frustration because I never got to finish what I started. But I had an epiphany one day after screaming to the universe when I realized that sometimes difficult people come into your life for a reason. They are the vehicles that help you change course. Sometimes we are unwilling to follow (i.e. too scared to take a risk) or unaware we should be on a different path in life. Many times we need a little push to see what's around the corner. It helps us figure out how we want to spend the rest of our lives, what message we want to convey with our actions. Cindy Key, a career strategist and friend of mine who is a Managing Partner in a company called Key Concepts, shared the following with me: "...clarity of message rarely comes as quickly as we wish it would...but when it does come together it is like the sun breaking out at about 10:00 A.M. on a foggy fall morning. The morning was thick and gray; the road is hard to see. You feel as if you are not sure where you are going and if you are on the right road. Then the sun jumps out, the color around you is bright, the grass is green and even if the pavement in front of you disappeared you are on the right road". Initially it may be difficult to figure out where you are in life, but if you approach your situation with the right mindset, you will eventually know where you are headed and what your purpose in this world is.

We all know that when they let you go the press release always mentions your win/loss record. But what it fails to mention is the undefeated record you have of helping young people and adding value to their lives. Ask yourself these two questions:

1. Did I make this place better by the time I left than it was when I arrived (added value to the institution I worked for)?

2. Did I do right by the kids (helped them develop on and off the court/prepared them for the real world)?

If your answer to both questions is yes you have nothing to be ashamed of. Hold your head high and move on to the next great endeavor that awaits you!

Chapter 20

THANKS, COACH!

These two words are all coaches ever want to hear from our kids. I always reminded my players that they needed to let people know they were grateful for what they were given--that they were not in their situation by chance. Someone, some people, cared enough to help them along the way. My high school math teacher Mrs. Kimbro is a perfect example.

> "You do the right thing for someone else without expecting them to do anything in return, and eventually the good you did will come back to you."

She took an interest in me when she found out I had no parents. Every day she would check in with me to see if things were okay. If I needed lunch money she would help me out. If I needed an ear she was there. She was only my teacher for one year but has continued to give me moral support throughout my entire career. Even after 30+ years we still keep in touch. Mrs. Kimbro empowered me, reminding me constantly that I was a hard worker and telling me I was smart. By her actions she was the first person to teach me the concept of "paying it forward". You do the right thing for someone else without expecting them to do anything in return, and eventually the good you did will come back to you. Her compassion and generosity changed my life and I promised myself that I would continue helping kids in order to pay her back.

I would never let my players complain. If they came into my office during the summer moaning about how hot it was my response would be "There's someone in Iraq or Afghanistan in a foxhole with full gear on in 100+ degree weather. *That* is hot. You should be thankful you have the freedom to walk around and do the things you are doing today". It has always been my belief that "please" and "thank you" are three of the most important words in any language. So whether it was a meal, some new gear, or a shorter practice, my message was to always give thanks. At first they would roll their eyes and say it begrudgingly. But eventually they began to do it automatically. And when people started complimenting them, it became a source of pride. I give thanks every day by keeping a book on a table next to my bed labeled "Blessings". Before I go to sleep every night I write down one thing that I am grateful for. It can be as simple as a sunny day or as heavy as a family member recovering from a serious illness. All that matters is that I recognize and acknowledge on a consistent basis the good things in my life and how fortunate I am.

Coaches love to hear those two words in another context--after our kids leave us. We are so happy when kids who come to us immature, not knowing what they don't know, depart as confident and prepared young adults. My favorite days are when a kid I coached calls and asks for my help or advice. I'm happy to know that my players still need me once in a while. Some of the players I used to coach are in the profession now and I really enjoy following their careers and mentoring them. Part of the reason I wrote this book is for them. I don't want them to have to struggle because they aren't aware of some of the simple things they can do to prolong and be successful in their careers.

When you coach you develop a lifelong bond with a kid. They may leave you after four years but you always want to know how they are doing in life. I swell with pride when a kid calls and tells me about her new job, love when she wants to have lunch to catch up and can't wait to hear about the exciting events in her life. And it's nice to reminisce and chuckle about the things you did for them that they are now old enough to understand. It's cool to know that they are using something you taught them with their own players or children.

It's great knowing I had some small part in helping the kids I coached become better people. I have fond memories of my time at Lenoir-Rhyne University, Wake

Forest University, University of South Florida, Western Michigan University, the US Naval Academy, Princeton University, and Merrimack College. At all those places I marveled at the creativity and ingenuity of the student-athletes. I saw them come in as freshmen with bright eyes and limitless potential and imagined the wonderful things they would be doing to lead this country in the future. I have no doubt that they will do things to change the world because of what they learned through sports.

    I also want to thank all the "coaches" who helped me become the person I am. Some coach athletic teams, some don't. The list of mentors, teachers, friends, coworkers, family and yes, even players is too long to print. I learned so much from them, whether I realized it or not at the time. Not one day passes without me using something they have taught me in some area of my life. So I hope my lessons never end. I hope I find more coaches who will help me learn new and interesting things about life and about myself. And I vow to continue sharing my passion for developing young people through sports with anybody who will listen.

    I encourage every coach to realize that coaching is about so much more than x's and o's; that participation in sports can be transformational. What we do has an enormous impact on the young men and women with whom we interact on a daily basis. We must understand that we also impact exponentially other people in this country. And recognize that, to some degree, we have an impact on the world in the way we help prepare our student-athletes as leaders. Most importantly, we should always remember that it is a privilege and an honor to participate in that process.

Resource Guide for Coaches

WEBSITES

Chronicle of Higher Education
www.chronicle.com

espnW
www.espn.go.com/espnw

espn
www.espn.go.com

Female Coaching Network
www.femalecoachingnetwork.com

Institute for Sport Coaching
www.instituteforsportcoaching.org

National Collegiate Athletic Association
www.ncaa.org

National Association of Collegiate Directors of Athletics
www.nacda.com

Women Leaders In College Sports
www.womenleadersincollegesports.org

Sports Careers Institute
www.sportscareersinstitute.com

BOOK LIST

7 Habits of Highly Effective People by Stephen Covey

A Bad Case of the Stripes by David Shannon

As A Man Thinketh by James Allen

As A Woman Thinketh
by James Allen and Dorothy Hulst

Coach Wooden One On One
by John Wooden and Jay Carty

Good To Great by Jim Collins

It's Your Ship by Michael Abrashoff

Leadership Is An Art by Max DePree

Man's Search For Meaning by Viktor Frankl

Oh, The Places You Can Go by Dr. Seuss

SuperRich: A Guide To Having It All
by Russell Simmons

The First 90 Days by Michael Watkins

The Little Engine That Could by Watty Piper

Water The Bamboo by Greg Bell

Who Moved My Cheese by Spencer Johnson

ABOUT THE AUTHOR...

Helen Williams has risen above personal tragedy to successfully pursue her passion for sports. Following the death of her adoptive parents at a young age she pursued her dual love of basketball and academics, walking on the basketball team and graduating with a Bachelor of Science degree in Health Science from Wake Forest University. She then received a Master's Degree in Counselor Education from Lenoir-Rhyne University. Her mothers, teachers, coaches, teammates, and mentors have all helped her form a values based philosophy that she uses in every area of her life.

In over 25 years in athletics Helen has built an eclectic and unique resume, spending time at Division I, II, and III institutions; Lenoir-Rhyne University, Wake Forest University, University of South Florida, Western Michigan University, US Naval Academy, Princeton University, Merrimack College, Massachusetts Institute of Technology, and Harvard University.

Helen's mission is to engage coaches and help them understand their roles in the lives of the young people they work with. Her company HMW Sports Consulting supports coaches by helping them achieve greater organizational awareness and enhanced professional competency, ensuring increased success.

HMW SPORTS CONSULTING

HMW Sports Consulting offers administrators a resource to support their coaches and help them navigate the 21st century intercollegiate landscape. By investing in your human capital with continuing education, you will save financial capital in the long run as you keep small issues from morphing into crises. My specialty is working with young/new head coaches and assistant coaches to prepare them to succeed as their careers progress. Using my extensive, unique resume with experience at Division I, II, and III institutions (Lenoir-Rhyne University, Wake Forest University, University of South Florida, Western Michigan University, US Naval Academy, Princeton University, Merrimack College, MIT, and Harvard University) I provide coaches with a foundation of leadership, management, and communications principles that enhance their master skill set and contribute to sustained departmental success.
http://www.hmwsportsconsulting.com/

SERVICES:
Customized Group Seminars
Departmental Coach Curriculum Development
Program Analysis
Individual Coach Development

www.ingramcontent.com/pod-product-compliance
Lightning Source LLC
Chambersburg PA
CBHW060527100426
42743CB00009B/1451